The Really Useful Donkey Company

By

John Stirling

ISBN: 978-1-9163789-2-6

2

Published By: -

i2i
PUBLISHING

i2i Publishing. Manchester.
www.i2ipublishing.co.uk

In memory of Michael Elliott, a brilliant director, who inspired me as a child actor in many plays at the BBC and in later life, production projects in both theatre and television. A huge lover of donkeys, the Michael Elliott Trust was established in the form of the Actors' Donkey Sanctuary. The aims were to bring these gentle animals back to life, so they could enhance the lives of children with special needs. As a result, wonderful experiences were achieved for many donkeys and children alike.

Acknowledgements

The Michael Elliott Trust, known as the Actors' Donkey Sanctuary, became one of the most successful animal theatre charities and children's centres in this country.

There were many people who contributed to that success and Annie and I would like to make special mention of the following;

The Artists

We would like to pay tribute to those artists who have given their time, money and expertise to the sanctuary so great.

The important people we need to mention are June Brown MBE, (President) and Dame Judi Dench, (Vice President); Georgina Andrews; Anthony Andrews; Lord Attenborough; Alan Bates MBE; Brian Blessed; Chris de Burgh; Marti Caine; Brian Cox; Michael Denison CBE; Sacha Distel; Marianne Elliott; Jean Fergusson; Edward Fox OBE; Lesley Garrett; Michel le Grand; Dulcie Gray CBE; Trevor Griffiths; Sir Alec Guinness KBE; Patricia Hayes OBE; Bill Kenwright CBE; Mark Knopfler; Hayley Mills; Sir John Mills KBE; Lord Puttnam; Jenny Seagrove; Martin Shaw; Michael Williams and Barbara Windsor MBE.

Without you all, the sanctuary would not have been established nor have run for so many years.

We would also like to mention Andrew Lloyd Webber owner of The Really Useful Theatre Company. This name was in our minds when we came up with the title of this book.

The Foundation

Mention must be made of the Flicka Foundation who so generously took in all my donkeys and gave them a life that they could have never dreamt of.

As we shall see, after over two decades running the sanctuary, it was time for me and my wife Annie to shift the focus of our energies and efforts. In a mutually beneficial arrangements, Flicka were willing and able to take our donkeys and provide excellent care of their health and overall welfare, while we continued to generate funds to help keep the foundation going.

The donkeys are all so happy in donkey heaven in Cornwall, so I dedicate the book to everyone at Flicka and of course, my four-legged friends.

To make a donation to the Flicka Foundation, please go to: https://www.flickafoundation.org.uk/donate.html

The Illustrator

We would also like to mention Ryan Sherwood who produced the marvellous animated pictures of the donkeys that you will see at the start of each chapter in the book.

Ryan has been a tremendous friend and supporter of the sanctuary and our work with the donkeys over a twenty-year period.

He has never charged me for his work.

Ryan Sherwood is a great talent and has always been a good friend to the donkeys, a friendship represented by his lovely illustrations in this book.

Thank you one and all,

John and Annie Stirling.

An all-star cast of remarkable donkeys give the performance of their lives to enhance the welfare and happiness of children with special needs.

Contents

Prologue

The Actors' Donkey Sanctuary

The curtain went up and the show began.

What a first night it was, when thirty of this country's most brilliant actors and directors came together to honour one of the very best producers, Michael Elliott OBE. This incredible company of artists got together with one aim, to rescue the animal that Michael loved - the donkey.

The idea was to bring these gentle animals back to life, so they could enhance the lives of children with special needs. This event built the barns for the donkeys' rehabilitation and the farmhouse for the children's therapeutic stays.

In the early days, things built up slowly. It was the case of taking in one donkey at a time and as the word began to spread about our work, the calls seeking our help came from a variety of places and circumstances, as we shall see. Once we had established ourselves, we evolved our operation so that we could set ourselves a guideline target of taking in three new donkeys a month.

Initially, we did much of the work running the sanctuary and looking after the donkeys ourselves. Soon, our efforts were supplemented by volunteers and ultimately, we hired full-time staff.

We also had to develop relationships with all the important people who could help us actually look after the health and welfare of the donkeys like vets and farriers.

The other key part of the sanctuary's mission was providing a place which could be used by organisations who looked after children with all sorts of disabilities. There were plenty of these organisations in and around the Peak District itself and in Derbyshire overall. However, although we had the idea of helping disabled children, we had to learn exactly what we could promise and what we couldn't as far as the children and the donkeys. How could we bring together young children with a wide range of disabilities alongside donkeys who also had a range of personalities.

We wanted to create good experiences, but the welfare of

the children and the donkeys had to be ensured at all times. As we shall see in the stories below, we began to understand that the donkeys each had their own personalities and gradually, the process began of allocating certain donkeys to certain types of activity. Of course, sometimes, this planned process was taken out of our hands, as in a number of situations, connections were made between the donkeys and the children which were a complete, although pleasurable, surprise to us.

Where possible, we encouraged the children to take part in caring for the donkey of their choice and this might involve various tasks, ranging from stroking and grooming their friend to helping with some of the basic tasks in the stables themselves, like filling the hay baskets and sweeping out any mess.

Most of the time, the children visited the donkeys in the sanctuary. Occasionally, some stayed in the special accommodation we had available in the farmhouse. On occasions though, we took the donkeys to the children especially if they were too sick to visit us.

Some of the donkeys also became part of our efforts to raise awareness and promote the sanctuary and this included times when certain donkeys accompanied me when I was making presentations or giving talks about what we were doing.

We also did special walks to raise money and these included a coast-to-cost walk from Scarborough to Blackpool with five children and five donkeys, looked after on the way, by my wife Annie and her sister, Linda and another long walk from Balmoral to Buckingham Palace, at the end of which Annie and I met Her Majesty Queen Elisabeth II, a very proud moment.

Another aspect of this activity was considering the needs of the children's parents who were experiencing the stress and worry of ensuring that their sick children were being looked after. Parental needs were always a priority.

We also developed the sanctuary from the visitor's perspective. Signs were put up in the local area informing people of our whereabouts. We then opened a shop on the site selling all sorts of merchandise about the donkeys. Annie also opened a tea shop which became incredibly popular and not just from visitors to the sanctuary but from tourists and residents in the local area alike.

Over the years that it was open, the donkeys themselves had become the integral part of the sanctuary and its life and not just due to them being there but through the contributions they made interacting with visitors to the sanctuary, especially the disabled children. Taking up and fulfilling such an involved role was a critical factor in helping the sanctuary to become one of the most successful animal theatre charities and children's centres in this country.

While our charity was called the Michael Elliott Trust, and the sanctuary itself, the Actor's Donkey Sanctuary, I've called the book *The Really Useful Donkey Company* as it reflects what these wonderful beasts actually did. It was not just their existence which was celebrated but what their contribution.

So what follows is exactly that, the stories of some of the amazing donkeys who we had with us at the sanctuary and their personalities, interactions and impact on those who came into contact with them. Each chapter relates how they made their way to the sanctuary, often saved from perilous circumstances, then becoming the focal point for the sanctuary's visitors.

In many cases, as we shall see, the donkeys developed touching relationships with disabled children from many organisations in the Peak District and beyond. The donkeys often helped to bring about major changes in the children's behaviour, confidence and self-esteem. In short, the donkeys became major contributors to the children's lives,

I hope you enjoy reading about these stories. I intend them to be a touching and often moving record of the sanctuary and its work made possible by the amazing donkeys themselves and what they achieved with their young, disabled friends.

Chapter 1

Baz

A TV star in the making

Baz was born in 1972 into a mining family. His father Bartholomew was a pit donkey whose job was to pull laden coal carts to a collection point, deep underground. He worked with his friend Benji for twelve years until the colliery was finally closed, when they were both brought to the surface for retirement. Their eyes were covered for several days, enabling them to adjust, gradually to daylight. It had been expected that Baz would follow in his father's hoof-steps, but instead, was sold to a scrap dealer and spent his teenage years dragging all forms of heavy metal across the yard to the crushers. He wore a heavy leather harness made for a much bigger horse and in the five years, it was never removed day or night, eventually eating into his skin causing severe infection and making him too weak to work. So, he was sent to market in Macclesfield for sale as pet food, a frightening experience and he was making everyone aware he was too young to die.

I was filming in Chelford for television and was completely taken aback at the state of the donkeys, penned and terrified. My wife fell in love with Baz. So that was that, Baz came home to live with us and recover. Baz took to show business like a duck to water. Despite all the hate and pain in his past, he was affectionate and calm, with a donkey-sized ego, ready to be let loose on an unsuspecting public.

Baz started his new career with the BBC and starred in an episode of *Challenge Anneka* where Anneka built him his own stables. He was then asked to join the one and only Muffin the Mule on *Pebble Mill at One*, which he loved. This was followed by a show called *Timewatch* which delved into Baz's work with special needs children. This led to his long-term friendship with June Brown, appearing in her Christmas video of *Little Donkey* and with her on *Songs of Praise*. Then we got a request from *The Tweenies*. They wanted to visit the farm and do a show, with Baz as their special guest, an offer he couldn't refuse, not only for himself, but for all the children who adored *The Tweenies* almost as much as he did! His most high-profile appearance must be when *Coronation Street* asked if he would do a scene with Curly Watts. Curly needed someone to practise his proposal speech to Raquel, so Baz was auditioned and looked suitably bored as the director wanted! Baz has appeared in theatres all over the country promoting his work with special needs children and continued to do so well as he entered his dotage! Baz has earned his place as the Artistic Director of this company, a role he undertakes with true professionalism for his fan club of children whom he now lives to please.

The Jack of Hearts

There comes a moment in everybody's life when something unexpected happens and remains in our thoughts forever. They are rare, but oh, so welcome. A donkey was about to experience and take part in something very special that only the quiet calm of an animal is capable of producing.

Baz had just appeared in the BBC programme *Timewatch* and was at home getting his hooves back on the ground, returning to normal life with his colleagues when two days after the programme's transmission, a large jiffy bag arrived addressed to BAZ. He had gathered an extensive number of fan cards over the years, but this was special. Inside the parcel were six wonderful pencil sketches of him in different situations; driving a cart, eating from his hay net, rolling in his sand pit; all lovely portraits of Baz, enjoying his life in the meadow. All the paintings were extremely well drawn, this was someone with talent, and we all wanted to find the artist. There was no address, but we were looking for an artist of some quality. Then, we spotted a clue. On the back of the last portrait there was a name - Phoebe, with the inscription, 'You are My Jack of Hearts,' nothing more, just that!

Baz now made it clear to everyone - he was on a mission! He needed all the help he could muster to find the source of this treasured gift. The answer came several days later with a letter from Phoebe, asking if it would be possible for her to meet Baz? Phoebe said that she would also have to bring her entourage, which would be three. A letter was sent back on Baz's personalized notepaper to let her know that he couldn't wait to meet her. Now everyone at the sanctuary waited in anticipation for the following Thursday afternoon, when the meeting was to take place. Baz was bathed and brushed with his mane plaited, revealing his large champagne coloured ears - which Phoebe had taken so much trouble to emphasis in her sketches. A minibus arrived at two o'clock, on the dot. Two people got out, went to the rear and started carefully lowering a ramp, down which came a wheelchair. The helpers adjusted things and made sure that the occupant was fine. Cushions were placed in strategic places for comfort and the oxygen mask was checked. Seeing Baz waiting patiently at the big barn doors, a little wave came from the chair acknowledging his welcome.

The wheelchair slowly got to the barn, it was at this point that Baz met the occupant, a very small young lady, pale in features but with the biggest smile Baz had ever seen. That smile shone so brightly that everybody around was taken aback by the affection so visibly radiating between her and 'Her Jack of Hearts'. Baz stood motionless, believing, as he always did, that he should allow people to come to him. This was tricky as there were medical accessories to consider, but Baz was good at caution and, after all, calmness was his middle name.

One of the ladies introduced herself as Phoebe's carer from the Manchester Hospice for children, then Phoebe introduced herself, already showing great maturity and personality for her eleven years. "Hi Baz, I've been looking forward to this so much." "I think we'll start with Baz's stable, as he would love to show Phoebe where he lives," I suggested, and everybody moved through the big green doors into the main barn.

"Here's Baz's stable. You will note that he already has all your lovely pictures around his wall making sure everybody can see and enjoy them as much as he does." Another large smile came over Phoebe's face. "There's a lot more where they came from," she laughed.

Phoebe's mother, an attractive lady in her early thirties, wanted Phoebe to get the most from life but was concerned about the effort of an outing. She had so much to worry about whilst living with the knowledge that life, in Phoebe's case, was likely to be short! None of these things seem to be bothering her daughter, whose full focus was on Baz; her eyes never left him. Baz now made his move, carefully closing in on the wheelchair to say hello to his new friend. The carers stepped forward worrying about the consequences, but they need not have worried. Baz remained firm insisting that he be allowed to share the experience.

Phoebe spent well over her appointed time in the stables until tiredness forced her back to the minibus. It was explained that her illness was a form of muscular dystrophy, and over exertion was a major problem. Although she had already managed to exceed her life expectancy, the muscles were gradually breaking down, and the last phase would be the heart and lungs.

Phoebe made twelve more visits, one a month for a year. Baz gave her a replica of himself in grey fur and this little donkey travelled everywhere with her. It even went (in a plastic bag) to the bathroom for showers and slept by her side every night; a real friendship of great value and importance to both of them had developed. Finally, the dreaded day came and after a month when his dearest friend didn't come to visit, Baz seemed to know, and it was noticeable to those who know him well.

A while later, her mother told us that Phoebe's last wish was for her fur Baz to be laid to rest with her. Loves last gift is remembrance.

Phoebe's pictures continued to take up the wall space in Baz's stable and unlike all the other donkeys, he never attempted, ever, to pull one down. They would be there for his lifetime and he made sure of that.

Chapter 2

Beethoven

Annie falls in love

Beethoven spent the first four years of his life living wild on the bleak moors of Derbyshire. It is believed that his mother had been turned out and left to roam with no help or contact with anyone. When she died, he was left to fend for himself and instinctively made his way to civilisation seeking food. Beethoven spent a week on the outskirts of an isolated farm sheltering by the dry-stone walls. When no-one claimed him, the farmer asked the RSPCA to remove him and they took him to a compound in Derby. He then received all the treatment he desperately needed, good food, de-lousing, and the trimming of his over-long hooves; but the important thing was he was given a name - Timothy. Re-homing him wasn't easy, as he was still a stallion, not the easiest of beasts, especially when other donkeys were nearby. After four months, he was placed with a couple who lived and worked on the land in Derbyshire. He seemed to like being a near neighbour to the Duke of Devonshire and began behaving like an aristocrat which didn't go well with the other occupant of the meadow including Arthur, who was also a stallion but had been a resident for much longer. The fights between them grew excessive, and we believe it was one of these battles that caused Timothy's deafness. Something had to be done, as it became apparent one of them could be seriously hurt. However, about this time the owners got divorced, the property was split up and Timothy ended up at Nottingham meat market. He was uncontrollable in the stalls trying to reach the Jennies who were lined up for auction.

He had to be moved to an isolated part of the market from which he escaped twice! On the second attempt, my wife Annie, caught him and eventually calmed him down. We soon realised; he was a lovely, handsome donkey with an affectionate but determined nature. My wife decided there and then that this handsome beast was not going to become pet food. As there were no bidders for him, due to his volatile nature, we brought him home, and he was renamed Beethoven.

Beethoven and friends walked to Assisi on his pilgrimage to visit the Crypt of Saint Francis, in northern Italy. While they walked, the support team drove the horsebox and enjoyed all Ludwig van Beethoven's classical music on CD. We loved it and it is such a shame our Beethoven couldn't hear it.

Michel Le Grand, Sacha Distel, the Swingle Singers and Vince Hill, all featured among his friends. Beethoven also worked hard for his charity, which seemed to make a very special donkey very happy.

A Small Miracle

When he arrived, Beethoven was still a stallion and we had over thirty female donkeys, so the first priority was an important surgical procedure! Within a week, he had recovered and was ready (and safer) to meet all his fellow donkeys. He was calmer and soon became enormously popular at the sanctuary. He had a natural aptitude with children and seemed to know instinctively what to do and what not to do. He enjoyed their company and was always very keen to make their therapeutic days as enjoyable as possible. Within a couple of months, he had gathered together an enthusiastic following, his own gang, all doting on his every expression and loving their special sessions. One child became very attached to Beethoven and a bond grew between them.

Nathan was twelve and had been in care for three years after being abused and neglected by his mother. He felt alone and disadvantaged but his care home had done a wonderful job of building his confidence and seeing his subsequent improvement at school, they decided to keep him in care a bit longer.

As a result of his fortnightly visits to Beethoven, he had become keen to learn more about donkeys, so Nathan borrowed a book entitled *A Small Miracle* from the library.

It was the story of a small boy called Pepito and his donkey Violetta who both lived together in Assisi, in Italy. It was the town made famous by St. Francis the patron saint of all animals.

Pepito had to make his own way in life after his mother passed away and his father, an American GI, had returned to the USA. In northern Italy, after the World War Two, things were tough, so Violetta and Pepito relied on each other, doing jobs around Assisi to earn a meagre living. One day, Violetta became ill and Pepito, frantic with worry, went to the local priest for advice.

He could not afford medicine, but he knew if he could get Violetta down into the crypt of Saint Francis for a blessing, the saint would make the donkey better. However, the stairs were too steep, so Pepito made a long pilgrimage to Rome. All alone, he waited for three days on the steps of the Vatican and eventually, the Pope took pity and granted the boy an audience. As a result, a wall was demolished, making room for the donkey to get down to the crypt and Violetta recovered. Nathan carried this book around in his back pocket - the library never got it back!

One day, Nathan asked us if he could take Beethoven to Assisi to retrace Pepito's steps. We were sympathetic but torn between the difficulties in organising such a journey and the safety of all concerned. After weeks of deliberation, it was decided that the idea and the project was so good that every attempt should be made to make it happen.

Several of our Patrons got together and bought a horsebox, a four star 'hotel' for Beethoven, Nathan and the team. The journey would take ten days in total with a three-day stop in Assisi. We went from Portsmouth by ferry to St. Malo, through France, over the border into Italy and down to Assisi.

We set off in the first week of September. The ferry crossing was nine hours, and our first overnight stop was a small village on the outskirts of Saint Rochelle. Beethoven was delighted that the farm had a female donkey named Cerise. He fell in love immediately but sadly had to leave his French lady all too soon! For the rest of the journey, we stayed in the horsebox which had beds, kitchen and every comfort you could wish for.

After four days, we arrived in Assisi which took Nathan's breath away. A glorious walled town on a hill, with the sun beating down, it looked like a picture postcard, exactly like the images in Nathan's book which was still in his back pocket. The following morning, Beethoven and Nathan began their pilgrimage to the Basilica. Nathan just found the whole experience unbelievable; it was like walking into his book. The tiny cobbled streets, the alley ways, the church bells, it was all just so important to him. Beethoven was also having a lovely time being admired by everyone around because, although this was the home of Saint Francis, very few animals visited!

Arriving at the church was a dream come true. Nathan and Beethoven were met by the Franciscan monks who care for the crypt. The monks where thrilled to see them both but were concerned that the donkey might slip on the stone steps into the crypt. Nathan took the reins, and slowly and very carefully they went together.

So it was, that a thirteen-year-old boy made a dream come true for himself and his donkey and showed the world what can be done if you just persist and believe. Nathan's motto was always 'Never Take No for an Answer,' and Beethoven would say, "I hope Nathan doesn't feel disadvantaged anymore!"

Chapter 3

Tinker

Destination Holmfirth

An extraordinary donkey, a real star and our greatest
ambassador, small in frame and very Irish, Tinker was born on a
farm four miles outside West Port in Southern Ireland. He only
had three months with his mother before being taken away. He
was sent to Athenry to join the herd of donkeys who work in the
peat bogs. He was just the right size: small, firm, well built, and
strong. The peat bogs had extremely difficult marsh conditions,
not only did the donkeys have to pull more than their body
weight but through sticky mud. After three arduous years they
were replaced by a tractor and the donkeys were shipped to
England, where they would get a good price at market. Tinker's
destination was the Holmfirth meat market in Yorkshire.

He now had lot number sixty-nine glued on his back and
was in the auction ring to be sold for meat or farm work. He was
having a horrible time, with the stewards hitting him so he
would move and show he was not lame. By chance, there was an
actress there buying a horse for her godchild, but the thought
that this pretty donkey could become pet food, was too much for
her. The price kept rising, but she kept going until the little
donkey was safe. The actress in question was a member of the
long running series *Last of the Summer Wine* which was filmed in
and around Holmfirth. The cast rallied round in admiration for
what she had done, especially as the market is a notoriously
unpleasant experience, especially for a refined lady in an
imitation fur coat!

Tinker arrived at the sanctuary which fortunately was
only a short journey from Holmfirth and immediately showed a
very special aptitude for working with children. He especially
loved going for walks and would test the children's endurance
by the distances he liked to cover. However, this could prove
difficult as he didn't like rivers, wouldn't cross bridges, didn't like
traffic, was unhappy near cattle or horses and had a particular
aversion to red letter boxes, cyclists and manhole covers. His first
sponsored walk was thirty-six miles from Sheffield to Buxton, a

two-day journey with a group of special needs eleven-year olds. He then joined in the coast-to-coast walk from Scarborough to Blackpool, a long trek over eight days, accompanied by his special young friend who lacked confidence and was terribly shy. It was thought this experience would bring her out of herself and it certainly worked!

Once back at the farm, Tinker was unwell, and the vet diagnosed cancer which had to be dealt with immediately. Tinker fought hard for many months as lumps and a tumour were removed, and he even underwent chemotherapy. To our sheer joy, he finally recovered fully.

A year later, to celebrate his courage, he went on his biggest expedition, with my wife Annie. They travelled from Balmoral Castle, leaving on Her Majesty's real birthday and in six weeks walked the many miles to Buckingham Palace, arriving in time for the Queen's official birthday and Trooping the Colour. They were asked to go to the Royal Mews then to Tinker's surprise, the gates opened and Tinker, along with Annie, went into the palace garden for a forty-five-minute private audience with the Queen where he received beautifully sliced carrots from Her Majesty. That was not the end of the story, as the Queen agreed that Tinker should feature in her Christmas message, as it was to celebrate the Commonwealth and its children. Her Majesty believed he would be enjoyed. So, from the peat bogs of Ireland to the Queen's private garden, has to be a very special journey, especially for a donkey! Finally, reading about Tinker's hard upbringing in Ireland, a young girl contacted us, asking if he could walk through Ireland with her so she could show him what Ireland really had to offer. So, Tinker's last walk was in his homeland, a full circle starting at Galway Bay and crossing Ireland. They were feted by everyone, a massive show of kindness and affection from a nation. He actually walked on to Manchester with Karen and a concert was given in their honour by Irish superstar, Chris de Burgh.

Tinker continued into his thirties and was still very active, working hard with his children, both able-bodied and special needs which he loved. That's our Tinker!

One more mile to go

The instinct for survival is a strong and personal experience. An encounter in Tinker's life brought two very different characters together, creating an opportunity for them to form a unique friendship.

Special needs is a very broad canvas covering many children's lives, but to categorise Tommy with that label was wrong. Just into his teenage years, he was able-bodied with an instinctive, raw intelligence; although his pale underweight body made him look vulnerable.

Tommy lived in a notoriously tough and dangerous suburb of Sheffield. His mother was an alcoholic, his elder sister was her carer, but stress was making her violent and uncaring, like her mother. His father had left when Tommy was five and has never been seen since. The electricity and water remained on, but the damp had now got a hold on the whole premises, leaving Tommy and his family with permanent chest complaints that were rarely attended to. Tommy had become adept at avoiding social services and their attempts to sort things out. He took himself to school and was doing well despite the obstacles and disinterest of his family.

Tommy spent his evenings roaming around the city centre, mostly avoiding home life. It was the week before Christmas, and he was walking down Ecclesall Road in Sheffield towards the new Waitrose shopping centre. He would stand in the doorway to take advantage of the heat, which blew out as customers went into the store. On this particular evening, there was a crowd near the doors, and he noticed that two people were standing beside a small brown and white donkey, resplendent in a multi-coloured, crocheted blanket and a head collar decorated with rosettes. Tommy wanted to get nearer and share the experience. A voice shouted over to him rattling a collection tin,

"Come and say hello to Tinker." Tommy hadn't got anything to put in the tin but wanted very much to go over. Another shout, "Come on don't worry about money, it's Christmas and it's children he wants to meet!" Tommy slowly moved closer until he was beside the donkey. Tinker scrutinised him carefully, his ears remaining firmly upright, an indication that everything was okay. Tommy felt a warm glow and stroked him many times, enjoying the feel of his thick coat. He patted him on the back and a cloud of dust rose. "That's alright," said the handler, That's how he washes himself, he rolls in the dust." Tommy was oblivious of time and after an hour, the man and woman started to pack up Tinker's belongings, ready for the drive home. "He'll be here again tomorrow," they promised, as they led him away.

The next day, he was at the store, waiting for the arrival of his new friend who arrived precisely at four o'clock. Tinker's helpers were pleased to see him and asked Tommy to lead Tinker slowly out of the trailer, which the little donkey seemed quite comfortable with. The helpers introduced themselves. They were working at the Donkey Trust over Christmas to help with the Carol Concert which was taking place the next day at the sanctuary. "Why don't you come to our concert tomorrow? Tinker will be there, with all his friends." "I won't be able to get there", Tommy said sadly. The man could see how much Tommy really wanted to be there, so he said, "Tell you what. Tomorrow, we will be here until six o'clock and then we'll go back for the concert. If you come here, you can look after Tinker in his trailer and enjoy the concert, then I'll bring you back as I live in Sheffield." The deal was done, with a huge hug for Tinker. The pair had seen what the donkey meant to him, but they had also made a note of how Tommy was dressed and appeared, physically. And so, Tommy was introduced to Tinker's world and this introduction would change his life. He stayed with Tinker all evening, he sang carols, cut up all the carrots that people were leaving for his donkey and gave him all the polo mints that were being donated. In fact, the staff, noting that Tinker was slowly filling up to the brim, had to step in. "I think that's enough Tommy, he'll keep going until he bursts, so best to stop now or you can clear it all up!" he said, smiling at Tommy who laughed out loud; he had never had so much fun. Three weeks later, when the snow had gone, and the roads were passable, Tommy was back to see Tinker. "You know Tommy," said the sanctuary manager, "Tinker likes a good walk. Would you like to do one together? If we bring Tinker to Sheffield, would you two do a charity walk back, which will help all the donkeys? It's a long walk, so we'll make it a weekend."

Halfway, they stayed the night at the *Poachers Arms* in Hathersage, then on Sunday, completed the journey to the farm. Annie went with them, so they didn't get lost and to make sure they were safe.

The walk itself was tremendously successful on many fronts; Tinker and Tommy bonded well over the two days; money was raised for the sanctuary and Annie noticed Tommy was a natural entertainer, singing and telling Tinker jokes. It was suggested that Tommy go to the Sheffield drama school to learn the trade.

Supporters, impressed by the walk and Tommy's love for his donkey, gave money for his fees which they called Tinker's bursary. Tinker and Tommy did more walks over the years, raising large sums of money for the trust and to say thanks to Tommy's supporters. Over the years, Tommy has also repaid Tinker by appearing in many stage-shows around the country, giving thousands of pounds to the sanctuary! But through all of this, it is important to end by going back to the beginning. Tommy's attempts at reconciliation with his mother and sister were fraught with problems and despite every effort, he was rejected, as he had been during his childhood.

Again, Tommy's strength came through and now, many years later, Tommy had a lovely wife and an adorable daughter Charlotte. Of course, there was one introduction that the proud parents couldn't wait to make, so Charlotte was introduced to

Tinker at two weeks old and visited the sanctuary most weekends. When Tommy's car came up the one-mile lane to the farm, Tinker knew the sound of the engine, and trotted over to the main gate ready to greet his favourite family.

Chapter 4

Bergerac

Facing retirement

Donkeys have come into our society as a domestic farm animal, working hard with a stubborn but lovable temperament, making their appeal universal. It is sometimes difficult to remember their history, coming from a very different background with their closest relative, the camel, with whom they shared miles of undulating sands in Arabia and across the Middle East.

This story was based nearer to home. We were in Saint Helier, capital of Jersey in the Channel Islands; a bustling seaside town with a picturesque port and a golden sandy beach. It was eight o'clock in the morning, shops were beginning to open, the locals were starting their day, as the high street started to fill with people. A sound could be heard, a distinctive noise the residents seemed take for granted. Down the main street came two very large donkeys, one brown and one grey. They were walking at a steady pace almost in unison, the bells on their head collars warning pedestrians they were on their way. Neither donkey needed a lead rope, as they made their way from their overnight meadows to the beach. The occasional polo mint was gratefully accepted from tourists, but there was always a short delay outside the greengrocers as they received two carrots and an apple each, just to keep them going.

Shopkeepers gladly told visitors of the day the donkeys blocked the high street for a whole morning unaware that the greengrocer was ill and unable to open up! Onwards they went to the beach, stopping the busy morning traffic, as these two were not going to wait to cross the promenade. They continued down the slope onto the sands and over to their working place, halfway down the beach beside the rock pools and sheltered by the high harbour wall.

The daily routine meant the grey donkey gave the rides, while the brown one, who had been ill, stayed with his friend for company but occasionally wandered off as a public relations exercise, to attract visitors to come and have a ride. It has to be stated at this point that the grey donkey would not go on the beach without his partner, the result of a twenty-four-year firm friendship that few could match.

Their fortunes were about to change as the beach had been taken over by a film crew and cast with a very large mobile catering lorry. The smell of bacon sandwiches wafted into the air. The whole television set up was deliberately close to the animals working area as they started filming an episode of the BBC's long running successful detective series *Bergerac*.

The grey donkey started his day, twenty-two paces forwards and twenty-two back. A crowd gathered as the filming attracted both locals and tourists. The actors made a big fuss of the donkeys with titbits from their travelling restaurant as, due to the rain showers they had long waits for the sun to come out again. With time on their hands, the actors begin to realise the donkeys had no breaks, no food or water. By mid-afternoon, the grey donkey looked weary, by evening, he was visibly very tired.

This went on all week as the filming continued and the actors became more and more concerned. On their last evening at the hotel, the dinner conversation turned to the donkeys, and someone said that the owner was about to retire these two donkeys to get some younger ones. So, the actors clubbed together and bought the two aged donkeys so they could retire with dignity. The animals travelled back to the mainland on the ferry, then from Weymouth on to Derbyshire and the Actors' Donkey Sanctuary where they settled in for their retirement. On the ferry, the grey donkey was named Bergerac and the brown one, Nettles, after the actor who played the famous detective. The final point, after twenty years at the sanctuary, and well into his forties, Bergerac still only walked twenty-two paces before turning around. A slightly surreal experience when he took the young special needs children out for a very strange walk!

The sands of time

Bergerac was a beach donkey, although the sand had been taken from under his hooves! He had worked the beach at Saint Helier for nineteen years and had given pleasure to many hundreds of locals and holiday makers, who enjoyed travelling twenty-two paces there and back. At times, his owner was unkind to him and he went hungry, but it was his life and like all donkeys, he just loved the people.

Karen was an eleven-year-old who lived in Jersey. Her parents had been killed in an accident leaving her to be looked after by her aunt and uncle who lived in Saint Helier. It had obviously been an extremely difficult time for them all, but the young girl found a lot of solace with Bergerac. His ability to listen was therapeutic and went a long way in helping Karen cope with her heartbreak. Her schoolwork improved and her confidence grew. The elderly couple were concerned that Karen wasn't making friends at school, but she explained that her best friend was on the beach, so every day, they made certain, come rain or shine, that she got to see her donkey. She missed Bergerac so much after he retired to the mainland that she made it her ambition to find him and visit him wherever he was.

Karen never rode Bergerac, although she often accompanied him backwards and forwards twenty-two paces, talking to him, and stroking his mane. They became real friends with an affection few people can understand unless they experience it themselves.

Karen was bereft when Bergerac moved to England although, being a sensible child and having witnessed the heavy weights that he often had to carry, she accepted, with great sadness, that it was in his best interest.

Karen was now fifteen years-old with exams taking up most of her time. She was determined to do well and go to university. She did well and then fortunately, her aunt and uncle decided to move back to the mainland to live in the Cotswolds, enabling her to go to university in England. Jersey had played a big part in her life, but she was originally from England, was glad to be home and hoped to meet Bergerac again

Karen finally reached the Actors' Donkey Sanctuary on a July afternoon. The sun was hot and the donkeys, including Bergerac and his pal Bramble, were shading in the wood. Karen went through the gate and down towards the herd, a big grey head rose from eating grass watching the oncoming human. His ears straightened. He moved slowly forward. Suddenly, Karen came into view and he was able to focus on her. Now he moved quicker and then, they were back together again.

Bergerac had forgotten nothing and was as ecstatic to see her as she was to see him. Tears were running down her cheeks as she rushed over to him. Now she had found him, she had no intention of losing him again. Karen was now studying law at Glasgow University but travelled down every month to see 'her boy'.

On one visit, Karen noticed that Bergerac rolled a lot and pawed the ground a lot with his hoof. The staff explained that he was still a beach donkey at heart, so she set to work getting him his own sand pit which he loved. He would be first out in the morning when the sand was at its best! Although he had to share this newly acquired piece of desert with fifty others, they were never as keen as him and he did manage to spend a lot of time by himself. Karen went one step further and raised enough money to build a riding ring with a sand base so he could take very young children for short rides – of just twenty-two steps each way.

Karen got her law degree but there was only one person important enough to show her graduation photo too. The staff at the sanctuary were very proud of her and spent a lot of time decorating her riding ring with bunting and flags and laid on a special cream tea. Karen had no idea that everybody was going to so much trouble. Bergerac had been washed and had his mane plaited. It was a big day for them both, and we wanted to show our appreciation for what she had done. Although the sand was for Bergerac, the riding ring also benefited hundreds of special needs children.

Chapter 5

Harry and Lettuce

A surprise discovery

The Staffordshire moors could be very bleak in winter, but many people moved there, searching for that escape to the country. Near a village, about thirteen miles from Leek, was a remote but beautiful farmhouse standing alone at the end of a long dirt track. It still needed extensive repairs as the previous owners ran out of money and had to move away, but a couple from Manchester left the suburbs of Cheadle to buy it. They saw the farm in autumn, but they were moving in during winter and it has been snowing heavily.

The cold wind had drifted snow against the dry-stone walls making the route to the house even harder and the landscape white and featureless. Getting services like heating oil and refuse collections would be impossible for now; even the post or shopping deliveries were out of the question. "You're on your own," said their nearest neighbour when they collected the key. The couple carried their two young children across the yard to the relative warmth of the house, followed by the provisions they had bought, preparing for a 'lock in'.

The house took time to warm up, and over the weekend the cleaning and unpacking started. It hadn't been possible to explore outside, but the family's wire-haired terrier had to, through necessity! After one of the dog's expedition, she seemed unhappy; almost scared of something out in the yard. Every outing saw him go to exactly the same place. His persistence alerted them that he had found something; oh please - not a rat! The snow was as high as the wall, and it was impossible to get near the place he was growling at, but the man did notice something worrying, the snow has formed a strange mound. On closer inspection he was sure he could hear something. He got a shovel and started digging. There was something under the snow, then a noise, then suddenly a snort of breath hit the frozen air. Finally, they saw frozen fur and heard a faint bray.

Completely taken aback and with no one near to help they dug and finally freed a large black donkey from his icy prison.

They tried to help him move to the yard a short distance, but he wouldn't move, just stared at the snow behind him. They didn't know why, until more tremors came from the snow, and they realised there was another donkey who could not get out. They dug hard until, there in front of them stood two freezing cold, starving donkeys.

When their shock subsided, they realised that they had to get them under cover, putting them in the old outhouse kitchen which was due to be rebuilt. Watching these two sad animals try and get warm the couple began to get very upset as they realised the previous owners must have left them outside, without a word to anyone, to just fend for themselves.

The outhouse kitchen became a permanent home for the donkeys through the winter, but initially, they lived on the remnants from the couples' larder as they still couldn't get hay delivered. Donkeys are herbivores, and it was very difficult for them to eat and digest spaghetti! Eventually, the snow melted, and the two donkeys went back in the paddock, but with access to their kitchen which they had grown to like! The young children were thrilled with their new friends and had many wonderful hours playing but this country retreat couldn't be a permanent home yet, it needed too much investment. So, both parents continued to work long hours and the farm would, for now, become a weekend retreat. The donkeys were now part of the family but needed care. Could the trust look after them?

As soon as the donkeys arrived at the Actors' Donkey Sanctuary, it was obvious, they were special. Their vet inspections told us the black male was about nine years-old, but his girlfriend was in her early twenties; so, she had a toy boy who was quite obviously mad about her! With their wonderful random thinking, the children had named them Harry and Lettuce.

Harry had a natural ability to work and play with special needs children. We didn't need to train him at all, he worked magnificently with both blind and deaf children. He had a natural intuition and a lovely temperament. I wish I could say the same about Lettuce who preferred talking to our adult visitors, she was, after all, a more mature lady! In true actors' tradition, Harry was a pantomime actor who loved children, while Lettuce was more late-night cabaret!

The Prince's Trust

St. James' Palace, London. A request from the Prince of Wales' office to the Actors' Donkey Sanctuary. His Royal Highness was attempting to find projects enabling groups of disadvantaged children to train and be able to get future employment. The scheme was being sponsored by Sainsbury's in the hope that the youngsters might be offered full time work.

The young people were joined by twelve able-bodied volunteers from the Prince's Trust who would oversee and assist in getting the project completed. The selected teenagers had to create a plan which would benefit society and charities and as part of this, the team had to be self-sufficient.

So, thirteen children from Sheffield picked the Actors' Donkey Sanctuary as their project and decided to build double fences around the meadows to safeguard the animals and allow the special needs children to enjoy their stays in greater safety. The first task was to finance the project and buy all the fencing, along with the nuts, bolts, gates and wire to fence thirty-nine acres of land and enclose a wood. With the help of our volunteers, the teenagers raised the seven thousand pounds by doing collections, open days, and car boot sales. Sainsbury's gave all the food, tools and safety equipment the children needed for their month's stay in our meadows, and the Prince's Trust arranged tents, stoves and sleeping bags.

Everything arrived at the farm and the tents were erected in one of the meadows.

During the first evening, guitars could be heard but, in the daytime, problems arose which no-one had anticipated. During the day, the donkeys shared the meadows, as until the fences were built, they have all the farm to roam around. The temporary toilets were quickly moved to the car park, so no-one was at risk of getting knocked over! The tents had to be secured, as they were prime targets for inquisitive donkeys who had never seen such things before. The pegs holding the tents down were excellent scratching posts and one donkey, Harry, who was used to going in and out of a house, had a new ambition: to enter a tent and investigate.

He always chose the same one to the annoyance of the two occupants. Every day, Harry took his sweetheart, Lettuce to the tent and attempted entry, but obviously he was too big and ended up flattening the whole thing. Even though the teenagers moved the tent several times, Harry's built-in compass never failed to track them down.

The two youngsters finally saw the funny side to things and become rather attached to the donkeys, who had already picked them out as friends and were not going to be put off.

As work commenced, the youngsters found out how hard it was to build the fences. Firstly, the holes had to be dug and the concrete mixed, and carried across the rough grass, for the wooden fence poles to be secured. Simon, whose new best friends were Harry and Lettuce, asked if it would be possible for the donkeys to help by carrying the concrete. We worked out what weight would be acceptable, and buckets were found so the donkeys could help, which they enjoyed immensely, because they were very intelligent animals and loved having something to do. Harry became very adept at getting the concrete delivered without spilling any. Harry also tried to get Lettuce motivated to work, but she was not keen. She thought manual work was beneath her, so Harry had a job on his hands. Lettuce would often just walk beside him, refusing to even carry an empty bucket! Harry was losing patience and the following day we noticed that Lettuce was grazing at the far end of meadow, while Harry had another lady with him, Rosie. The two worked well together all day but trouble was brewing as Lettuce became jealous but couldn't get through to Harry as the young team had already completed one meadow and she was cut off behind the new fence. She made many attempts to get through, but the fence held well. At the end of the day, it was sad to see Harry get so much earache from an irate Lettuce.

The following day Harry was ready for work and Lettuce joined in, anxiously waiting for her first bucket of concrete. Rosie, on the other hand stood by the fence watching.

Some of the team said she was smiling; did Harry have a co-conspirator?

The month was soon over, and the tents came down. The youngsters had enjoyed working and playing with the donkeys and a few of them had made really good friends with them. The donkeys too, were sad to see everything packed up, but their fields were beautifully fenced and safe, peace and quiet returned to the meadows.

The Prince's Trust were thrilled at the successful outcome of the project and when his Royal Highness came to Sheffield, he made a point of mentioning this work, which demonstrated his delight that the children and volunteers had done so well in keeping to their mandate.

Harry's new friend Simon got a fulltime job at Sainsbury's and is now a fully trained fishmonger, but Harry is disappointed he didn't choose the fruit and veg. What pleased his Royal Highness was that every youngster got full employment from the project, so the Prince's Trust also achieved its goal.

Simon visited the trust regularly and was never slow to let people know who gave him the greatest inspiration. Harry and Lettuce became part of his life and when he brought his own daughter, she was absolutely spellbound by daddy's special friends. Lettuce, however, whenever she spotted Simon, was delighted he hadn't come to work as she now felt that if Harry suggested that again, she would have to put her hoof down, very firmly!

Chapter 6

Thistle

The performer's mascot

Thistle's parents Sebastian and Bippy were born just outside Sunderland, within a mile of the shipyards. Their owners had a guest house, 'Roker View,' right on the cliffs overlooking the North Sea. The guest house was well known in the area for its connections with the arts and show business and was one of L. S. Lowry's favourite haunts. He would spend hours on the cliff top, drawing and painting, creating his unique image of this hard-working environment.

The North East had the biggest club circuit in England spreading from Sunderland to Newcastle and all the outlying districts. In each town, there were thriving working men's clubs. Venues like *The Scala Nightclub, The Miners' Social Club* and scores of others, seating hundreds of people every cabaret night. It was usual to heckle many of the acts, but those who did well could just stay in the area and make a very good living, playing the same clubs all-year-round. The one type of act that the punters really liked were groups, as they were less likely to get booed off. Strippers were also well received, but not by the acts that had to follow them!

'Roker View' had a deal with a local club and many of the acts stayed there. The owners didn't mind if the artists didn't get up until about two in the afternoon, as they usually played two clubs a night and then had to pack up all their gear. It was usually quiet in the mornings unless Sebastian, Bippy and their foals decided to bray for attention! Many of the acts used to make sure they went to see the donkeys before going back to the noise and smoke of the clubs. It was like therapy, the donkeys calming them down, before a further onslaught.

All four donkeys were white, so very distinctive, and lived in a small paddock behind the guest house. Sebastian's claim to fame was that Lowry had included him in two of his pencil sketches which he later sent to the guest house as a present and they were proudly displayed in the dining room.

One boy band were regulars on the circuit and stayed at the

guest house four or five times a year. They took a liking to one of the foals – Thistle. He was a small two-year-old donkey; very affectionate and seemed to remember and like the boys whenever they stayed. He became their mascot and photos of Thistle were all over the van and even on the amplifiers when they were on stage. It became their trademark, to always dedicate their last number each night to Thistle.

Old Sebastian died, and sadly - as often happens with donkeys - Bippy followed only four months later, leaving the young donkeys alone.

About a year later, the guest house was sold, but the new owners were not donkey lovers and decided to put them up for sale. On their next visit, the boys were devastated that they might not see Thistle again so asked if they could buy him. The four lads all came from Wigan and Robert, the lead guitarist, persuaded his mum and dad to give Thistle a home in their paddock.

However, they were advised to take both, as donkeys are not happy alone, they are herd animals. So, the boys bought Bernice as well, but without asking Robert's parents in case they refused!

Thistle and Bernice only had one more worry. Having bought both donkeys, the boys were now penniless and could not afford horsebox fees to get their new friends to Wigan. So, after a gig, they emptied their van and got the donkeys in the back. Not ideal but it was a big van and quite high, so it worked, and they got them safely to Wigan. Robert's parents actually pleased they had saved them both, and the two small white donkeys became great favourites.

Amy's wheelbarrow

Thistle was a happy donkey, he lived quietly with Bernice in an affluent home on the outskirts of Wigan, where the retired owners showered them with all the best carrots, sugar beet, hay and grass pellets. They were spoilt. As Spartacus the rooster brought in the dawn, Thistle would rise from his deep laid, unruffled straw bed, shake himself down and have a good stretch, sometimes even a roll on the dewy grass if he felt like it. Then, it was a gentle stroll over to his paddock gate, which he learnt to open two years ago, and across the patio to wait patiently to announce to his adoring owners that he was up, and it was time for breakfast. With a huge bray and a shake of his ears he banged on the bottom of the kitchen door for service. Mr and Mrs Brown were quick off the mark with his breakfast as they had already lost three kitchen doors to his over enthusiastic demands, or just simply that they hadn't moved quickly enough.

Thistle kept his hooves crossed that Evadne, the family Doberman, named after Mr Brown's mother, had not knocked the bucket off the kitchen table. Thistle was perpetually trying to convey his anxieties regarding the careless positioning of his morning treat.

One sunny morning in late spring, Thistle waited longer than usual for breakfast and was close to seriously damaging the kitchen door, when a stranger put his bucket out and closed the door immediately. This was not customary behaviour and although he finished in normal record-breaking time, he was concerned by the appearance of this new person. The lady came out again thirty minutes later, collected his bucket, returned him to his paddock, and locked the gate; something Thistle was not accustomed to.

There was a lot of cars arriving and leaving that morning, totally unsettling the donkeys' everyday life. Still, there was no sign of their owners. By tea-time, they were really hungry, and Thistle decided to bray and kick the gate until someone gave in and spoke to them. Robert Brown, their son who had bought the donkeys, arrived looking pale and anxious. As before, he was comforted by the calm nature of Thistle and told him that Mr and Mrs Brown had been killed in a traffic accident. Thistle sensed something was wrong but obviously was not able to really understand so he and Bernice just meandered back into the stable and settled down. Three days went by with no treats, just having to eat grass. That evening, Robert came over to the stable and put head collars on them both. He led them to a waiting trailer - this was not right! As ever, Bernice just did as she was told but Thistle was not going to leave the place and those he loved. It took them nearly two hours to get him into the trailer. He showed his anger by practically kicking the trailer walls out. He was frightened and did not want to go; also, he was desperate to see his owners who he had missed so much over the last few days.

The journey took just over two hours and when they arrived at the sanctuary, Thistle was sweating, he had cut himself in three places and the head collar was twisted round where he had tried to get out of it. He was in a terrible state. The ramp came down and the first person to step forward was Amy a young volunteer but very responsible and caring. Amy spent ages in the trailer calming him down and although he was by no means right, he was approachable now. Following the laid-back Bernice, he finally came down into the courtyard. He was fearful looking around nervously, until he noticed four heads looking over the drystone wall, and they appeared to be the same breed as him! One gave a loud bray, a welcome, easing Thistle's nerves a little. He brayed back, not loudly but enough. Thistle was led into a stable with thick straw up to his knees. There was plenty of water, a hay net in the corner and a bucket of pasture mix if he wanted it. Amy stayed with him until he settled. After a while, the breathing got less laboured and he tried some hay. Amy left, and as he rested his weary head on the stable door, she kissed his muzzle and wished him a good night. In the morning, Thistle awoke to an extraordinary sight, his stable was on the end of a row housing at least forty other donkeys, all getting themselves ready for the day. The donkeys passed his door on their way out to the meadows, some stopping and welcoming him, others sizing him up wondering what he was going to be like. People were bustling around but Amy was dealing with just him for his first week, to settle him in. She arrived pushing a wheelbarrow and started mucking him out. After a while, Amy was called away but when she went back to finish his stable off, surprisingly Thistle wouldn't let her back in, he was being defensive about something - but what? This went on all day and Amy became worried she could not even get her wheelbarrow out!

The sanctuary manager rang Robert Brown to see if he could shed any light on the problem, but he couldn't enlighten them, until he suddenly said, "You haven't by any chance been using a wheelbarrow around him, have you?" "Yes", he said "We use them all the time." "Ah, my father always left his wheelbarrow in the stable at night in case it rained. Thistle thought it was his and had been put there for him. To be honest, it was the love of his life. I'll tell you what, I will drive over at the weekend with the old barrow, it might help."

The wheelbarrow duly arrived, and Thistle had his old friend back, and Amy finally got her wheelbarrow back too, after a five-day siege.

Thistle and Amy were seldom apart, he adored her. They went for long walks and you will probably find this hard to believe but, yes - the wheelbarrow had to go too! It's quite extraordinary that this young girl was seen walking with her donkey, without head collar or rope, but having to push the blasted wheelbarrow, if she wanted him to go. Months of trying to wean him off it had come to nothing, so Amy had decorated it and given it the name Ron, after Mr Brown. Even though Thistle had a wonderful new friend, donkeys are extremely loyal, and he would never forget the couple who were kind and made his early years so happy.

Chapter 7

Emily and Elliott

A Star is Born

Kirkby Lonsdale in Cumbria and the last Friday of the month has traditionally, been market day. There was a lot more activity than usual when the Appleby Horse Fair was in progress nearby. Horses and carts were trotting briskly up and down the main road showing off their speed, whipped on by flamboyant men, mainly travellers, making sure the traders noted their horse. This was the annual sale and they wanted the best price for their beast. To show them as the fastest and the best left the animals somewhat abused and tired, upsetting at times, for the visitors watching the spectacle, unused to seeing horses, donkeys and ponies treated this way.

One animal causing great concern was a very overweight red and white donkey. She was attempting, with all her might, to do as instructed by a rather heartless driver, but she could not pull the weight. Beside the road was a diverse audience, some shouting at her, but a few horrified holiday makers showing their indignation at the driver. The donkey eventually collapsed, lying on her stomach with her legs folded under her. Eventually, two more men arrived, and the animal was dragged off the road onto the verge, as other carts and drivers were trying to get by.

The donkey was left on there, but they removed and took the valuable cart, effectively leaving her worthless. Two children standing with their parents, were crying, overwhelmed by such cruelty. They went to the donkey trying to calm her by stroking and talking to her but there was little response as the animal was hurting too much. The children begged their parents to so something. The parents were reluctant to get involved, this was no place for their children, and they attempted to get them away quickly. However, the youngsters would not move, and the girl sat down beside the donkey showing considerable understanding and affection. The animal was now sweating profusely but still unable to stand. At that moment, a police car went by and they flagged it down. As they did so, a large number of onlookers quickly disappeared! The policeman got out and surveyed the scene; they had had to deal with quite a few unpleasant incidents in the past few hours and this came as no surprise.

"We'll advise the duty vet and get him over here," he said. The parents did not want to give a description of the offenders and neither did any of the remaining crowd. It was the young girl, still kneeling by the donkey, who told the police what happened, much to her parents' concern. The police seemed to recognise the man from her detailed description. The donkey was now in great discomfort and groaning, trying to roll over to get off her stomach. As she managed to push herself over, someone noticed two small hooves protruding from her back end. "She's giving birth," he shouted, to everyone's horror.

It took several minutes before the duty vet arrived and took charge of the situation. He desperately needed a hand and astonishingly, the teenage girl showed no signs of anxiety or worries about what she was faced with and immediately did everything that he asked of her. About an hour later, she was able to sit back on the verge and survey her success - a very beautiful red and white foal which struggled immediately to stand by his mother.

The next problem for the vet was that the mare was so weak and tired, she couldn't stand and provide the foal his urgently needed first feed. The vet milked the mare and made a temporary feeding bottle from objects in his car. He asked the young girl to try and gently feed the foal to make sure he got all this very important first milk. "Had this donkey been on her own in this situation, neither of them would have survived. You must be very proud of your children, they are a credit to you," said the vet, to a rather bewildered but proud couple. "Thank you," said the father. "They have showed us a thing or two today."

Eventually, the mare got to her feet but not without some pain. She cleaned her foal from top to bottom and she was also coming around to being able to supply the milk herself which was a great relief to the vet. "Now we have to consider what is to be done with them both," he said.

The police had returned with the person they suspected, and the child instantly confirmed it was him. "Since hearing there was a foal involved, he was actually trying to get both animals back, because there was money to be made." "Well," said the vet, "That's over to you. My job is done but my report will emphasise that the condition of this animal was deplorable, and I don't think he should be able to retain these animals and that he is prosecuted." Then he turned to the young girl and her brother and said, "I firmly believe that these two youngsters should be commended for their actions." Those last words did not go unnoticed by the children, nor were they ever going to let their parents forget them.

The donkeys were not returned to the dealer but were taken to the safety of the Actors' Donkey Sanctuary, which was only eleven miles from the children's home. The mother donkey was named Emily after her young friend and her foal, we called Elliott. The children visited every week, took their donkeys for walks and thoroughly spoiled them. They were rare donkeys with their red and white colouring, so Elliott became a star and made many appearances on TV, but Emily was very much a home bird and liked nothing more than to be with her friends in the meadows but always with one eye on her actor son, who was quite a handful.

Chapter 8

Sable

Some Like it Hot

Sable was the most beautiful donkey, with dark brown fur that deepened almost to black around her eyes and on her soft muzzle. Beautiful yes, until she yawned or curled her lip up in pleasure at the sight of an extra strong mint. Sable had a jaw defect which is very common amongst the Sicilian miniature breed, which made it difficult for her to eat. Her front teeth protruded forward, making it very difficult for her to pull grass or hay. She had to rely on her back teeth to crunch everything to pulp and this led to digestive problems as the food didn't always get mashed up properly before being swallowed. Sable's teeth were causing concern so, for the first time, we went in search of an equine dentist. We found one in Ashbourne, but a man much in demand and for a very good reason. James was a miracle worker and a fine equine dentist. It didn't take long for him to deal with Sable, he had an extraordinary way of calming and talking to the donkey. Sable was classed as difficult by the farrier, the vet and others who had to deal with her but here, in a matter of minutes, she was under his spell. It has to be said that James was also a very handsome man with an immensely appealing manner, making my female grooms weak at the knees! But it's the way he approached the animals that was truly incredible. Sable seemed to realise that she had to behave, and James understood that Sable had certain foibles that had to be respected. Without any form of sedation and with instruments resembling giant files and claw hammers, James managed to work for an hour on Sable's teeth, removing the ones which were causing trouble and rasping down the sharp ones that were causing pain. At the end of each session, they were still friends. After the dentist had worked his magic, Sable was calmer, and her personality was totally transformed.

She also found herself a friend in Kojak, and to see this demure little donkey alongside the biggest, strongest donkey in the herd was a sight to behold. Like most giants, Kojak was a pussy cat and he adored Sable. He would do anything for her and would defend her honour to the end!

We didn't know how old Sable was, as the certificates were incorrect when they arrived here, but here again, our genius dentist could help. The way to determine the age of any equine is by the teeth and after a thorough investigation, James revealed that she is between nine and eleven. A young donkey!

Sable went on to be a glamour girl; was photographed by three eminent BBC wildlife photographers and appeared on the cover of two famous national magazines. She was painted twice by artists of great quality and the portraits sold for substantial amounts. One of the portraits was donated to the sanctuary and raised enough for a full year's hay – 1,800 bales at £7.50 a bale. I will leave you to work out the maths. Her image also adorned our shop on postcards and greeting cards. She even featured in an equine publication as an exceptionally pretty specimen of a miniature donkey. Good job we got her teeth fixed; I hear you say!

Finally, we had many offers for Sable - some quite astonishingly high in value but we always reassured her that when we promised her that she was here for life, that is what we meant. Was she perfect? Not quite. Her maternal instinct was non-existent, but she was as safe as houses here and we loved her dearly.

The donkey doctors

Sable redeemed herself over the years and made up for her lack of affection and maternal instincts towards her son Bobbin. It took time and effort to make her understand that she had a lot to offer and that glamour was not everything. Every month, the sanctuary attempted to rescue and home three donkeys. The phone calls came mainly from the police and private individuals who had witnessed something they wish they hadn't! For a donkey to be admitted to the trust, it had to need attention and specialist care, and our vets were trained for any injuries and were quick to respond. We had a special five-acre meadow with its own independent stable block, always ready with thick beds, hay nets and food buckets at the ready for that urgent call. The best initial treatment for a sick or injured donkey was another donkey, as they seemed best equipped to befriend and calm other animals down. Somehow, they had a mutual understanding that led to injured and traumatised animals getting back on their feet quicker than with any injections or medicines. With this in mind, we had two permanent companion donkeys who lived in Buttercup meadow, or the sick bay as we called it. Sable and Popcorn showed over and over again what could be done, and the results were outstanding. Consider the case of a mare in her twenties rescued by the Derbyshire police and brought to us in a horsebox. As the ramp went down, it was obvious from her injuries that she might not survive, but we would always try – they all deserved a chance. After two hours, we managed to almost carry her to the meadow, and we lay her down, exhausted, under the large oak tree which acted as shelter against the rain and shade if the sun was too hot. The vets were already there examining her. It was suggested that she was put to sleep immediately as the injuries were substantial and life expectancy was short.

The donkey had been kept in a small garage for two years standing deep in excrement, unable to move about, and with no windows, light or fresh air. She was too traumatised to bray, so nobody heard anything even though there were houses not too far away. It had been a terrible shock to the small community to realise such a violent act of cruelty was happening on their own doorstep.

As the vets went back to their cars to prepare the injections, Sable and Popcorn appeared, sensing their presence was required. Sable was the first to move close to the donkey, who was flat out and unable to even raise her head. A comprehensive sniff around the entire animal alerted Sable that all was not well at all. Popcorn went around the other side to investigate and as he did, the donkey twitched her tail, either as a defensive move or just pleased she was not alone. Sable licked her ears and around the muzzle. The head moved, appreciating this attention. Sable encouraged by this, carried on, now joined by Popcorn, who was gently prodding the patient's back with his muzzle. At this point, the vets returned with the lethal injection but were amazed at the sight of these two miniature donkeys nursing and encouraging the sick donkey. They also noted that although the donkey couldn't quite get up unaided, it was now showing enough alertness to give her another chance. Although we realised that this would mean someone being with her all day and night, if she was trying, so would we.

The vets suggested we gave her the weekend and they would return on Monday to see how things were. Obviously, if she got worse, the vets would be back immediately to put her out of her misery. Over the weekend, the weather was kind and so were Sable and Popcorn! They took their job very seriously, never leaving her alone; there was always one with her as they rotated their nursing schedule. She was not able to stand in the two days, but she got her legs into a proper lying position which lessened the pressure on her stomach. She had a gentle brush to remove some of the muck from her fur and had eaten a bucket of pasture mix and grass pellets, hand fed by a very patient Annie.

The vets arrived for their review on Monday morning and were astonished that she was on her feet with one miniature on either side of her helping her balance, but they were all still under the tree.

The vets were most delighted that she has been able to do her business which, to us seemed odd! Apparently, it signified she was ruminating which was good! She stood with the miniatures for just over an hour and then she lay back down again but this time she was able to rest properly. Popcorn was constantly licking her eyes and muzzle, so we realised that a fly fringe was needed as the flies are attacking her without her being able to fight them off. It took Sable and Popcorn two months to get Violetta back on her feet. They showed immense patience even sharing their buckets with her and making sure she was never alone in her stable. They were both overjoyed when she started to roll and, after weeks of trying, she made the complete roll from one side to the other and the two miniatures did a lap of honour round the meadow! People believe donkeys are stupid, but they are actually very intelligent, as this story has shown. Believe it or not, Violetta never had any medication in her three years at the sanctuary, thanks totally to Sable and Popcorn. This was just one of their success stories; both donkeys helped and encouraged many others who found life difficult, but to Sable and Popcorn that was not a language they understood!

Chapter 9

The Jersey Boys

Long-distance travellers

It was early Monday morning on the runway at Denver airport in Colorado. A cargo plane was preparing to take off for Brussels carrying sixty-nine Sicilian miniature donkeys in thirty-one wooden crates. These small donkeys had become fashionable and were bound for a lucrative auction at Macclesfield, in Cheshire, in three days' time. Two donkeys were in each crate to be safe and to keep warm, as the temperatures in the cargo hold could get very cold during this nine-hour flight. They were frightened by the powerful droning sound of the massive engines revving up to take off. Some of the donkeys were pregnant, others were with foals at foot. The rumbling of this heavy aircraft, as it gathered speed along the tarmac, was something they had never experienced. They didn't understand the intense noise and movement, they had no idea what was happening to them. During the long flight, they had little chance of moving. There was not enough water and no hay nets; nothing to ease the trauma, especially for the pregnant mares, who found it increasingly difficult having to remain static, not even able to turn around. The foals stopped feeding as they were so stressed. They finally landed at Brussels, but unfortunately, this was not the end of their ordeal, or their journey. The next morning, they were pushed out of their crates and into two lorries which took them through Europe for another six hours. Then came a ferry crossing from Calais to Dover, followed by yet another journey of five hours to Macclesfield. The transport company gave them minimum amounts of water and hay as they didn't want the bother of cleaning out the lorries more than necessary. For pregnant mares, this was not just cruel, it was dangerous.

The animals arrived at Macclesfield market; exhausted, nervous, unable to move properly as they were sore and stiff. The foals were shaking and in poor health. The last two Jack donkeys were in the lorry, sticking together like glue, one head on the other's shoulder, as if hugging each other. The dealers moved in and got them out with sticks, shouting to make the terrified animals move. The whole herd just stood together in one corner of the big pen erected specially to show them off for tomorrow's auction. The suggestion from the auctioneer was to leave them: "They need to find their legs and stop shaking otherwise you won't get a good price!" Everybody left the barn. The lights were turned off, leaving the animals in the dark, but after an hour, still none of them moved. Finally, during a cold night in the dark, they slowly started to move, with difficulty.

These tiny donkeys were left to contemplate their future, to feed their young and just to wait listlessly for the outcome of the auction, none of them sure that things were going to get better for them. The auction took place and most of them found new homes. However, there were five donkeys – including a mare with her tiny foal – who were so traumatised by the journey that they could not be sold. Luckily for them, one of our supporters was there and saved these little gems, and they went to live happily at the farm.

Chapter 10

Tickety-Boo and Cappuccino

The Four Seasons

Two of the little Americans or the Rat pack, as they were known to us, had a special role to play. They had been chosen for their versatility, personality and ability to make children happy and how they did it, we believed, was unique in the donkey world. Instead of working the orthodox way by allowing children to groom them, feed them and talk to them, these very special four liked to... Party! We noticed that Tickety-Boo and Cappuccino always came into the barn while the staff mucked out. It didn't matter how good the weather was or how lush the grass, if the music was blaring out from the barn, they wanted to be part of it! They seemed to have favourite tunes, orchestral themes and when they heard big band music, they would come and stand at the main gate, rocking with joy. So, we decided these must be musical donkeys. How could we turn that into something special for our children's parties? We would do special events four times a year for terminally ill children and either go out to their hospice or, if possible, they would come to us.

We devised the Four Seasons.

Winter Wonderland was a party where they visited a children's hospice. In the cold weather, it was much better for us to visit them, so our donkeys arrived in style in their Irish horsebox, bought for us by Chris de Burgh, the famous singer. We had speakers on the side of the lorry, so we were able to start the music as we entered, and the donkeys came down the ramp to *"A Winter's Tale"* by David Essex. They were dressed up for the occasion and would make their way to the specially cleared assembly hall ready to meet the children. The first item was a dance to the music of *"Agadoo."* Each donkey would have a child partner and they would step backwards and forwards in time to the music. Then we would follow this with a rousing version of *Little Donkey* which the children had already learnt but which our two seemed to think was their signature tune. Then presents were exchanged - bags of polo mints and carrots, all beautifully wrapped by the children themselves. In return, the donkeys would leave a selection of coloured pencils, chocolate donkeys and donkey crackers. The donkeys gave out special postcards of themselves – the only thing they could not do was sign them! Then it was back to the music. The winter party lasted only about thirty minutes, as most of the children were very ill and got tired quickly. It seemed so short, but we were reassured that the happiness the donkeys gave went a long way to make life a little easier.

The Summer party was easier, held outside with more to do in the fresh air, with the donkeys' ability to do the ordinary things that are expected of them. Rides were the most popular, and we had basket saddles made so that ALL the children got an equal chance. Tea, scones, cakes and buns were enjoyed and shared with their four-legged friends finishing up with some very happy, but tired children.

Autumn was a musical fair with stalls, tents and games. It was a family day when their parents joined in. Often coping with great stress, they could have reassuring teas with other parents and not feel they were the only ones. Watching their children enjoy the Jersey Boys' unique style, everybody said they had never seen donkeys like it. They hadn't expected that animals could generate such happiness for their youngsters, and it made it a very special time.

Spring was a joyous Easter celebration. The children were invited to church to see the minister bless the donkeys at this special time, always a moving service but often the mood was raised by one child asking, "Do you think the donkeys will poo in church?" and giggling. They never did but it would certainly have brightened up a few children's lives if they did! Then, to the church hall for a lovely Easter tea naturally with music and gifts.

So, that completed the Four Seasons' year. A very rewarding one but with a tinge of sadness that we had such a short time to entertain many of these brave children who taught us much more than we could ever teach them.

Chapter 11

Paphos and Sky

Saved by the filming

Cyprus was the choice for many holiday makers and British people wishing to live a different life in the sun. A wonderful island where to relax was to enjoy, but for some of the inhabitants, life was not quite so straightforward or clear cut. Outside the towns, in the hills and surrounding olive groves, farm life was very traditional. The tasks of the day were governed by the heat and the population was used to timing their chores accordingly, but for the animals, life was very different. The donkeys especially, had a hard life, as they were treated like machines; literally workhorses with little food and shelter. It was a common sight to pass a farm and see a donkey in the midday sun having to work an eight-hour day irrespective of the heat!

Retirement was not an option and life expectancy was short in these conditions. Donkeys, mules and some horses were regarded in the same class as cars or farm machinery. They were not a living thing. They were just there to do a job. The main anxiety, for those who cared, was that the animal was expendable and when they were too old or ill to work, they were pushed off a cliff to save any further inconvenience, and in most cases, cost!

In this situation were two young foals, whose mothers had been disposed of at the end of their working lives. One of the mothers survived the fall, but with a badly broken leg making walking almost impossible, her foal was left suffering. The foals would die of neglect, as they were too young to work and could not survive alone. Luckily, there was an animal rescue centre outside Paphos, and they came to the rescue, but time was short. What could be done to help these two young and healthy foals? On the island, a few miles along the coast, in the shadow of Aphrodite's rock, a film company was making an epic pirate spectacular with stars from Britain and America. On an inclement day, which rarely occurred in the summer, the cast and crew were given the day off to have a break. Two of the

British actors headed for the cool of the hills and came across the animal sanctuary. They heard about the young donkeys and a plan was hatched to get them to England where they could lead a useful life and be treated with dignity.

The actors got help from the British military base who quickly made suitable crates to safely transport two young donkeys on a flight to Manchester. The crates were finished in a day, but that is the type of help and efficiency you can come to expect from our forces. There were huge advantages to being what might be termed a famous face, and getting the flight sponsored was one bonus. The transport was now arranged, vet checks done and as there was no quarantine required, the only thing left was passports. So, they needed names and the actors choose one, Paphos and the RAF choose the other, Sky. The actors decided to travel with the donkeys and make sure they were met at the other end. As two of our supporters, they naturally sent them here, to the Actors' Donkey Sanctuary. As the actors flew straight back to the island to resume their filming, they kept very quiet about their great adventure which had meant a new life for two lovely, gentle and very deserving creatures.

Baz

Harry & Lettuce

Meeting the Queen

Paphos & Sky

Rhapsody & Blue

Sable

Tinker

Chapter 12

Rhapsody and Blue

Trams as heavy as a London bus

It was six in the morning and the working day was starting in Budapest, Hungary. After a hundred years of tradition, one mode of transport had changed.

Gone were the workhorses that pulled one of the cargo trams around the city and in their place, came two donkeys. The horses have been sold for meat as they were too expensive to maintain and now two big grey donkeys filled their place. The trams were like barges on wheels, designed to carry heavy loads to factories in the city. The horses used to work in shifts as it was heavy work. They would pull for two hours then rest; if a horse was too tired, it just would not work. Now, the two donkeys were expected to do the work without stopping. The owner was ruthless, there were few breaks in the daily routine, and although they were on metal rails, the trams weighed the same as a London bus!

The authorities started to get complaints from the general public, anxious at the sight of the two donkeys suffering, especially as parts of the journey were up hill. Eventually, one of the donkeys collapsed, leaving the second one to struggle against the drag and to stop the tram rolling backwards. The stricken donkey was dragged on his back for several metres before the driver eventually put the brake on; but even then, he didn't go to the aide of the animal! First, he checked that his cargo had not fallen out or been broken. He took the collapsed donkey out of the harness, leaving the second animal with the full weight as he took the brake off again. He whipped the sole donkey to carry on, leaving the first animal abandoned.

At the time, work was hard to find in Hungary and the driver was not in the slightest bit worried or concerned about the public's reactions and shouts of abuse. With no action taken by government officials, the man was left to his own devices. However, the public found their voice through the media, concerned that their country was being let down by this one cruel man. Some animal welfare workers approached a film company working in Budapest, and the camera crew offered to film one of these journeys and the trauma it caused the donkeys.

It worked! Eventually public pressure won, and the man was forced to stop using the donkeys. Unfortunately, the donkeys were now worthless, so they were just left in a field to fend for themselves. Thankfully, the film crew and the actors remembered them and now took control. The donkeys were flown to England and joined all the other donkeys at the Actors' Donkey Sanctuary.

The two Hungarian donkeys made themselves at home in Derbyshire, but their size worried the herd. They were, as donkeys went, enormous, thirteen hands and very strong, even after the abuse, poor diet and neglect. The two of them were now called Rhapsody and Blue and they turned out, after much tender loving care, to be the most handsome of animals. Due to their size, we were still wary of letting them work with children yet, but they were great favourites with the general public. As one lady said, "If he says it's Thursday... it's Thursday." – how true.

Chapter 13

Ebony

Saved from The Bunny Farm

In the hills, a few miles from Wrexham in North Wales, a couple had set up a visitor attraction called *The Bunny Farm*. As the name suggested, the place was full of rabbits, all shapes and sizes, living in converted chicken houses, left by the previous farmer. The owners were waiting for a licence to open, when for some reason, one day, they simply abandoned the farm and disappeared into thin air, never to be seen again. As they hadn't told anyone, their departure wasn't noticed for some time. No one realised that the animals had just been abandoned. They hadn't just left the four hundred rabbits but many other animals that the couple had accumulated; two horses, two donkeys, six goats, two sheep, some geese and chickens and a pot-bellied pig. Arriving at *The Bunny Farm* was a distressing sight. Many people believe all animals, if set free, will revert to being wild and be able to fend for themselves. This is so wrong! The rabbits had got out and as some breeds (especially the bucks) are hostile to others, there had been fierce fights, leaving dead and injured animals everywhere. The surviving rabbits were in a very ragged, hungry and dehydrated state, as the only water was provided by the odd rain shower. The two horses were lying dead in the field – obviously they hadn't starved in that short time, so the neglect must have been happening for some time.

The alarm had been raised by a neighbouring farmer, who became concerned by the distressed bleating of the sheep. He rescued them and the goats, while the chickens and geese had been rounded up and taken to a local poultry farm. The two donkeys were in the same field as the horses. When we arrived, they were standing alongside the bodies; how they had survived, no-one knows. They were certainly in terrible condition, coats matted and full of lice, fly bites and maggots round their eyes and their hooves so long, it made it extremely difficult for them to stand. Before loading the donkeys, we helped the RSPCA deal with the rabbits, who all had to be caught, boxed and loaded into a large van. It took all day and while we were doing that, our groom attended to our two frail donkeys, who didn't know what was going on. The horse carcasses were removed, and the donkeys showed visible distress that their one-time friends were being hauled away. Finally, we were able to load the donkeys in our trailer, after the vet had checked they were fit to travel. The vet was confident that it was a mother and her year-old foal. The mare was in her teens and by the look of her extended stomach she had been a brood mare, having had a foal every year so they could be sold for profit. The mare was dark brown, and a remarkably affectionate and friendly donkey despite her cruel treatment. However, she was totally exhausted having had to take care of her son, who was also completely emaciated.

We called the mare Ebony and her son Bramble, and living at the sanctuary, they soon recovered completely. The fact that Ebony could walk without pain, once her hooves were trimmed, gave her a completely different outlook on life. Bramble too, was enjoying donkey company and when another foal called Conker arrived, Bramble was over the moon. At last, a friend to play with! What was amazing was the way in which Ebony instinctively took Conker under her wing as well, as if he were her own. She liked looking after them both, protecting them from the older donkeys, who could be a little boisterous. Conker grew up alongside Bramble under the watchful eye of his foster mother, whom he adored. We get used to the foals leaving their mothers after a few months and never really having much contact, other than saying good morning! But Conker never left Ebony for more than short intervals, always returning to her to make sure she was still there and to feel secure. Her time as a brood mare was not in vain as there were very few donkeys who would be capable of giving such care to a young donkey who was not her own. Ebony also showed enormous sensitivity to children with special needs and had one of the longest lists of fans; she tackled it all with her unique maternal instinct shining through. It was hard sometimes, to think back to that awful scene, where two emaciated donkeys were left to die and how far these wonderful beasts came, bearing no grudges and bringing so much pleasure to so many.

The hills are alive with the sound of donkeys

Some of the children who stayed at the farm were not very mobile. One fourteen-year old named Tracey was so taken with Ebony's story and the fact we knew nothing about her, she made up this story for her:

'In a small hamlet just outside Shrewsbury is a breeding centre for donkeys. There is a small field, housing around twenty or so donkeys. Most in good condition except one who looks very tired and very pregnant. "She's been a wonderful mother," comes a voice standing in the cottage doorway. "We've had a few foals from that one, all good." It transpires that she is a brood mare and has produced thirteen foals in the same number of years. The donkey's name is Daisy. She is dark brown and about to deliver at any moment. Her shape gives the appearance of carrying panniers on each side, and she is flanked by two yearlings. One is her son Jamie and the other is Diesel her surrogate son, whose mother had died.

It is a hot day; in the corner of the field one large oak tree provides the only shade and several of the donkeys are lying beneath the tree under its green canopy. Daisy joins them, but unable to lie down for fear of not being able to get up again. The flies are bothering her. A young girl comes out of the farmhouse and takes over some carrots which Daisy enjoys and takes time crunching them up. The young girl is obviously attached to the donkey and sympathetic to her needs. She replenishes the water trough and an old hay net which hangs from the lower branches of the tree. Daisy is showing signs of discomfort and is stamping her feet and turning around and around in endless circles, letting everyone know that she is going to give birth very soon.

The young girl doesn't go for help, instead she gets close to Daisy and successfully calms her down. Next, she gets all the other donkeys up on their feet and away from the tree leaving Daisy to give birth in peace. Jamie and Diesel are reluctant to leave her but are finally convinced by the youngster. Daisy struggles hard and has considerable trouble delivering the foal. Her muscles are not what they used to be, and her strength is considerably sapped by the midday heat. She labours for some time to no effect and finally, she is forced to lie down with exhaustion. The young girl sees the problem but as there is no sign of the foal appearing, she can do nothing yet. She gets a bucket of water and gently pours some along the donkeys back to cool her. This seems to revive her a little and she gives another try. The girl is still concerned and rushes indoors for towels. As she covers the donkey in wet towels, the foal's hooves finally appear, and she is able to tie a leading rope round the hooves and start gently but forcefully to pull. After an hour of hard labour, the very large foal drops to the ground and Daisy wastes no time in cleaning her up and offering milk, so essential in the first hours. Daisy has performed superbly but has suffered greatly from this ordeal as she is now too old and tired to keep having foals.

However, this a breeding farm, and the owners will want to service her again in a very short time. The young girl takes it into her hands to ask for help and request that she be homed at the sanctuary, which is within travelling distance for her to keep in touch.

So, Daisy comes to Derbyshire to live at the sanctuary, with a new name Ebony. Visitors still ask if she is pregnant due to the fact that she has never been able to regain her figure, and she will always have the "saddle bags". She wouldn't come without her foal, so Ebony arrived at the trust with Bramble. Because of her natural aptitude with her own children, Ebony has turned out to be extremely popular with children. Always surrounded by youngsters she revels in their attention and affection. Her quiet nature is also appreciated by parents as she is the most patient of animals and exudes tender loving care to the smallest and most frail children. Last year we awarded her our 'Muffin the Mule' trophy for her work with special needs children, which is proudly displayed in the trust's shop - The Actors' Studio.'

Chapter 14

Compo

A TV star in the making

In 1998, a donkey escaped from Holmfirth livestock market and disappeared into the hills surrounding this picturesque Yorkshire town, better known as the location for the immensely popular TV series, *Last of the Summer Wine*. The donkey had been sent to market, so nobody wanted him, and no-one bothered to look for him. Sightings were reported near the reservoir and these often made the pages of the local paper, but the animal was in an ideal place. He had water to drink, meadow grass and ferns to eat, plus trees and hedge rows for shelter. Those who got a glimpse from afar said he looked in perfect condition, so it was apparent he was doing fine living in the wild.

One sunny afternoon, the cast of *Last of the Summer Wine* were scheduled to film a scene by the reservoir. The crew arrived early to set up the cameras, lights and sound on the location. The butty wagon provided breakfast for a hungry cast and crew. The four large caravans were ready to be used as dressing rooms by the actors participating in today's filming. The whole set resembled a wagon train in those fabulous old western movies. In the butty wagon, the chef had started cooking bacon and the aroma was drifting over the area. The chef thought he saw movement in the bushes behind his van. Suddenly a scream went up from one of the dressing room caravans as an actress was scared by the vision of a large hairy animal, peering through her window. She screamed and it disappeared!

The production manager was sent to find the creature before filming could commence but there was no sign of any animal. Filming began and the first scene was shot quite quickly. The series had been running for over twenty years, so everybody knew exactly what to do and how to do it. "Cut," shouted the director. "I'll just check the rushes before we go on to scene two," and off he went to his caravan. A few moments, later, he reappeared slightly bemused. "What's wrong?" asked the production manager. "During the whole scene, there's a large brown donkey in the background, some way away but the camera picks it up well. Although the scene is good, viewers will be transfixed by the donkey. It's a long way off but, you can't miss it, it's just standing there staring at camera as if it's in the scene which, of course it is! We will have to re-shoot the scene but get rid of that donkey?" That order was easier said than done. The donkey had done its Houdini trick again and completely disappeared. The crew combed the area but no sign of it, so it was considered safe to re-shoot the scene. The cameras re-focussed. The cast re-rehearsed and all was well. The weather was perfect and there were no planes going across to upset the sound boys.

The director said, "Action," when the cameraman noticed the donkey was back in exactly the same position with the same stance and the same expression. The director, in his utter frustration, suggested a quick re-write as the only way forward was to include the donkey in the scene and to make mention of it in the script. The donkey was obviously not going anywhere so he was inserted into the scene so they could get on. The next problem was that the donkey now followed the crew to the various other locations and was now making things very difficult unless the director wanted to turn the whole episode into a donkey serenade! He even appeared in the car park of the local hostelry after filming. In the end, enough was enough, the animal was caught by crew members and "brought in for questioning." Should he be handed over to the authorities? No, the actors wanted him to go to the nearby Actors' Donkey Sanctuary and they named him Compo after their principle actor Bill Owen's character. Compo began a wonderful life, working with special needs children which he loved. Sadly, Bill Owen passed away some years ago, but Compo continued to remind everyone of the days both he and Bill starred in the series, to keep the memory and the name alive.

There's a hole in my bucket

In Holmfirth, there are many tributes to the actors of the long running *Last of the Summer Wine*. There is a fish and chip shop bearing their names and tea rooms reminding people of who they were. There is still a guided tour that sets out most summer days, taking visitors to all the locations that are so well known. Several of the actors bought homes in and around the area. After all, they spent many months a year there and when the series ended, many of them stayed. Compo the donkey was named after the main character, who was brilliantly played by actor Bill Owen, who took his Yorkshire heritage seriously, always showing his true grit and determination but also opting for caution and great resilience. Whether he was frugal, we shall never know! Having become locals, the actors took part in many of the towns activities and enjoyed many community projects.

The local paper was delivered each week and read avidly to find out what was going on. In November, the paper carried a worrying story about a young girl of nine who went to help a pony in the auction market's car park. The small white pony had been transported to Holmfirth in a very old, rusty trailer pulled by an equally unsafe car. The driver had put the ramp of the trailer down to get the animal out, when it collapsed under the pony's weight. The pony's legs went straight through the boards and were stuck amongst the rusty frame.

The pony started to panic desperately trying to release itself, as it did so the tailgate fell off completely. No one seemed to know what to do or made any attempts to assist. The driver disappeared knowing he would have to face questions about no tax, insurance or MOT; the pony had to fend for itself.

Noticing a lot of blood around the pony's feet, a nine-year old girl named Maddy ran over to the trailer. People shouted at her to stay back and someone went into the market centre to find her parents. There was no way of calming the panicking animal, so Maddy's instincts told her to try and release it. She couldn't bear to see its terror. She had a pony herself but hadn't recognised the danger or strength of the pony. She fought to get its head collar off, which she succeeded in doing; then she managed to remove the broken boards but, as the animal sensed freedom, he reared, jumped and galloped away. However, he crashed against Maddy, knocking her off the tailgate onto the car park leaving her seriously hurt! Maddy was in hospital for some time with a severe head injury, sustained as she had fallen on the concrete. She was having trouble communicating and talking, she had also broken her left arm in four places along with an ankle but when she managed to speak, her first words were "How was the pony?" The pony had survived thanks to Maddy, but now, the question was how to get Maddy better. What was the outlook and outcome going to be? The Holmfirth actors asked if, when Maddy was ready, she could come and have time at the sanctuary's residential home. They thought, as she was so animal orientated, that time with our donkeys would be the best therapy, but after the accident would she now be wary of animals; the answer – no! This brave young lady jumped at the idea and, even though she was having trouble communicating, everyone could see this was something she would like to do, and it might help take her mind off the problems surrounding her at present.

Maddy came to stay, went in the barn and there was Compo, always nosey, wanting to know what was going on and why a new child was staying at the house. Maddy's bedroom was on the ground floor as stairs were tricky, and there was Compo outside. There's nothing quite like seeing a majestic donkey's head staring at you first thing in the morning! Was it fate that made Compo team up with, and help a young girl from Holmfirth? There are many strange things that we will never understand.

The doctors estimated that Maddy would probably need over a year to get back to any sort of normality but that hadn't included the Compo factor and she was back to school in half that time.

They were inseparable. She spent four months of her convalescence at the charity with him. Maddy brushed him every morning and they went for short walks every afternoon, and as she got stronger the walks got longer and longer until Compo had to put his hoof down. He started to turn around and head home because he was getting too tired. There are so many accounts of things the two did together, but it all amounted to one thing: a real love for each other. Finally, it was time to go home and back to school but, there was one thing which Maddy wanted to do with Compo by her side. She had found out that the pony who she tried to help back in Holmfirth had gone to a family just outside Glossop and she pleaded with us to take Compo with her to meet the pony again. They made the journey together and the sight of the brilliant white pony cantering round his paddock with hardly any signs of his ordeal made Maddy really happy. In typical Yorkshire fashion, Compo was stoic and quiet, taking it all in his stride, but Maddy never let go of his mane during the whole visit!

Chapter 15

Silkie

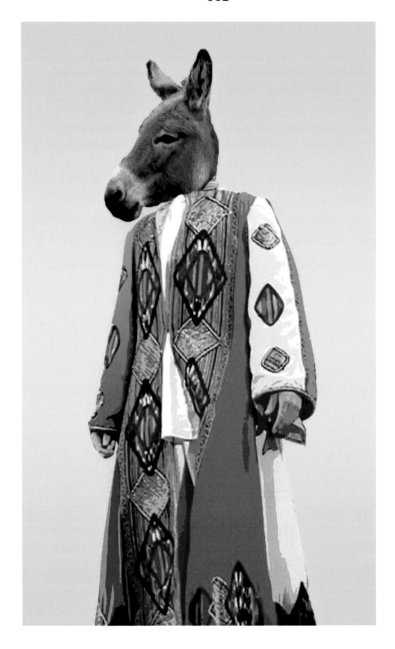

An exhausted American mum

The location was the Inky Dinky Donkey Farm in Ohio, US. Joseph Abraham Lincoln was their star stallion and his job was to sire as many Sicilian miniature donkeys as possible, as they were required for the markets in Europe. This was a task he took seriously and was very proficient at it, which made him an enormous asset to his commercially minded owners.

At the end of her breeding life, one of his mares - Violet, was flown to England for an auction at Macclesfield in Cheshire. Pedigree certificates showing Joseph as the sire were eagerly sought-after, the foals from his endeavours could reach thousands of pounds.

Sadly, Violet was in bad shape after the ordeal of her long journey from America, and she was declared unfit for sale. So, she was brought to the sanctuary where she was put in a stable to rest and prepare for the imminent arrival of her foal. Everybody kept their fingers crossed that she would manage the birth given the poor health she was in. The time came and when she tried hard to give birth, she just didn't have the strength. The foal was in danger of suffocating and it was left to the stable manager to assist in any way she could. All that was visible were two tiny hooves that wouldn't budge. Gradually and cautiously, the efforts of our staff showed signs of success, as bit by bit, the legs came into view and finally the foal was pulled out and dropped to the ground. Violet was too tired to even clean her, so the foal was washed by the staff and returned to Violet, hoping she could give her the milk she so desperately needed. Violet couldn't oblige as she was totally exhausted, leaning against the wall and finding it hard to stand, so we managed to milk her, and bottle feed the foal. The bottle feeding went on for three days while Violet recovered, then she was able to partly bring up the young one herself, although the foal was equally attached to her human family.

The foal was named Silkie and it became equally reliant on its human contact as its mother's efforts. Silkie actually preferred to be looked after by her carer which left Violet with more health problems, as she couldn't get rid of her milk and missed being maternal to her foal.

Silkie was always been convinced that her mother was our manager and not the donkey. This meant she always had a tendency, whenever possible, to get close to people rather than animals and she would always leave the herd if children and adults come to visit.

The reaction from the general public was always the same. "What's the name of the little donkey that has just followed us all round the meadows?" they asked. The answer was always the same, Silkie! She was absolutely brilliant with her young wards and did the most terrific job with them, regarding herself very much as one of them. None of us wanted to deter her from that feeling, or the work she so enjoyed.

The nativity coats

The sanctuary was based at a farm high up in the Peak District. Winters could be hard with the Derbyshire winds whipping in and persistent rain. Frequently, snow blocked us in, but for all of us, would come the moment we all looked forward to - Christmas and there was nowhere on earth that we would rather have been, than sharing this special occasion with our wonderful donkeys.

A few weeks before Christmas was when the donkeys realised that something special was about to happen. The donkeys who had been at the sanctuary for a few years recognised the signs, as the 167-foot barn was transformed into a magical place. The anticipation was written on their faces and Silkie was no exception. Coming up to her fifth Christmas at the sanctuary, she was beginning to know the routine and how it all transpired.

In Manchester, the head window dresser at the leading store, Kendals, was having a rethink for her Christmas displays, both inside and outside the shop. As she decided on the new theme, she had to consider what to do with the multitude of old decorations she no longer needed. Fortunately for the sanctuary, this lady sponsored Silkie and made an offer which we could not refuse; could we use their old decorations? At first, none of us were aware of what that entailed until two huge lorries arrived and unloaded enough decorations to cover half the village. There were massive Christmas rings made of straw, trees of all colours with the most lavish lighting systems. Seasonal characters, the seven dwarfs, Cinderella and her coach, Aladdin and his lamp and all sorts of animals all lit, culminating in the most beautiful nativity scene. The delivery took four men from Kendal's three hours to unload and for us, it took a week to decorate the barn but, when it was completed, it looked magnificent. Even the donkeys were staring around at the colours especially as they had to live in these lavish surroundings for a while.

At this point, we must not forget the enormous input our senior citizens put into our trust each year, their tireless efforts, always divided equally between the animals and the children. They packed and sold our Christmas cards; helped make our boxes of unique crackers and worked tirelessly to decorate the barn. Then there was the ladies' speciality, knitting and making the coloured nativity coats for the donkeys. Every year in the village halls, the church halls and the community centres, the ladies of Derbyshire made each donkey a new Christmas jacket. It was an undertaking that took two months, but they never failed the donkeys. So, the middle Saturday of December was the carol concert, 'The True Meaning of Christmas'. The barn looked superb, and the nativity coats were a highlight of the proceedings. The ladies were always so careful that all the squares were a different colour and the effect when all the donkeys were lined up in their boxes, all beautifully turned out, was a sight to behold and never failed to get a gasp of approval when the visitors entered.

The local school choir took its place on the straw bales, supported by the *Manchester Students' Orchestra*, ready to sing all their favourite carols, that we all joined in but as the announcement said, no clapping at the end of each carol as that made the donkeys a little frightened.

The local bell-ringers heralded the arrival of Father Christmas, who rode in a coach pulled by two trusted donkeys: Baz and Kojak. Suggestions from some that they should wear antlers did not go down well, and the fact that they trampled on them made quite sure they were not going to look stupid! After Father Christmas delivered presents to our special needs' friends, the *Pantonic All Stars Steel Orchestra* played; these talented teenagers played brilliantly. Visitors mingled, had a go at the games, bought last minute presents from our shop and fed the donkeys from the carrot buckets. Just before everyone left for home, our Chaplain gave a reading and a blessing. Silkie was brought forward and blessed each year as she was born at Christmas, so she embodied the whole proceedings and was the donkeys' representative on this special occasion.

Chapter 16

Annie

Surviving in donkey hell

Annie was the very first rescue and probably the hardest. Everything was new and we couldn't believe that animals could be treated in this way. It doesn't matter how many stories you read in the papers or how many news programmes or documentaries you watch, nothing prepares you for the real thing.

It began on an estate in Stockport, a few miles outside Manchester. The police called the sanctuary to warn us that they were making an arrest but, before they did so, they needed the donkey at the centre of the abuse to be collected and taken somewhere safe. The location was a lock up garage at the end of a row of terraced houses which led on to fields where some old, unkempt and neglected horses were grazing.

The garage itself was small and shabby with no windows. There was no sound coming from inside. The police were able to break the door open and as they did so, the smell from within was unbelievable. It was a fairly long garage and once inside, there was a shape visible at the end, crouching by the back wall. To get to the animal, it was necessary to wade, literally knee deep, in excrement. There was a small, white donkey. She was frightened and not used to seeing the daylight, as apparently the owner only came at night, when he was confident no-one was around. She could not move, and we had no idea how long she had been in that position. It was difficult for the vet to examine her, as he couldn't see properly, and he couldn't move her outside. He immediately knew she had broken ribs on both sides and a badly bruised stomach that he assumed were from kicking and beating. There were other marks and healed scars on her back and rump suggesting more beatings! Word spread on the estate and the police had to set up a cordon to keep people back. It was a difficult area that could erupt easily at a visible police presence, but the sight of the donkey made them sympathetic and calm.

It took an hour to bring the donkey out. She was hardly able to stand on firm ground, so the vet gave her a sedative so we could transport her safely. The police took many photographs and made notes so a prosecution could be brought but there was still the matter of the owner. It turned out, he was a solicitor's clerk in Stockport, who weighed over twenty stone. A couple of the locals finally admitted they had seen him trying to ride the donkey, which was in itself, hardly believable, as she was so small, but that was a while ago and they thought the donkey had gone. He lived with his elderly mother and what everyone found astonishing, especially those who lived nearest the garages, no one could recall ever hearing any noise and yet, it was estimated she had been there for a couple of years! For us, even facing this man was an unpleasant experience. The arresting officer had trouble with him because he knew the law well, from his job. However, with the police and the vet to help, we got the donkey into our horsebox and away. The prosecution went ahead but it took nearly four months before the sanctuary was given total ownership and Annie was legally safe forever.

The man got a seventy-five-pound fine and told never to own any more animals. The sanctuary's cost exceeded two thousand pounds, but we couldn't get any of that back.

The sun will come out tomorrow

Annie's wounds still took time to heal. She had to have a metal plate in her rump to enable her to stand correctly after years of cowering in that awful garage. Her ribs mended and her stomach, although still visibly large, were bearable for her. Her back was badly dipped which left her with severe arthritis. You may ask, "Why didn't you put her to sleep?" I will tell you why. With the care and dedication of our expert staff, Annie enjoyed a peaceful, happy life at her own pace. She made donkey friends and she gave joy and happiness to hundreds of special needs children and hundreds of human visitors over the years. She was a remarkable animal who bore no grudge towards anyone; even her previous owner who attempted to visit her and argued to have her back!

Katherine was eleven when her teacher, at the Buxton Community School asked us, gently, if we could help. She wondered, if we could give this very shy, nervous child, a weekend job. The reason was, she was having severe problems coping with a broken family and other domestic complications, and she needed time away from that environment. Katherine was not doing well at school and was underachieving in most subjects except art, where she did brilliant sketches of animals.

Katherine was invited to visit the sanctuary, to see if it was the sort of place she would feel at home. She arrived with her teacher who was very supportive and obviously concerned that the child was finding life so difficult. The teacher explained that Katherine was being bullied at home and she felt the best thing was to try and remove her from that situation and encourage her to be more self-assured and confident.

Katherine's eyes nearly popped out of her head as she saw the barn full of donkeys of all colours, shapes and sizes and all looking over their stable doors to welcome her. She walked along the passageway, reading their names and their reasons for being at the sanctuary, finally stopping at the end stable - the only one with no head looking over. The name was clearly printed on the door, Annie. Kath lifted herself up to see over the top and there was Annie lying down in deep straw having a rest. The donkey's head lifted up in acknowledgement of the girl's effort to see her. Kath read the story and was deeply moved as was her teacher and the girl asked if she could go in. Permission was given and our staff and the teacher enjoyed a mug of tea, leaving the two to get to know each other. An incredible bond was set that afternoon in the two hours they spent together. Annie got up on her feet and it was very clear that these two had struck up a valuable friendship and one that was to last for many years to come.

Kath was only thirteen years old, but we invited her to work weekends and soon she was also working in the holidays, half-term, and any other time she could get to the farm. When Kath arrived at the stables, all the donkeys would bray and welcome her as if she was a long-lost friend. She visited Annie whenever she could and the two would spend many, many hours together. In fact, the staff had to be pretty strict to get her to go home, sometimes pushing her into a car and driving her away to make sure she actually went home. Kath just wanted to be with her 'best friend in the entire world', as she put it.

At school, she did better, not brilliantly, as Kath was never going to be an academic genius. But Annie played a big part in improving Kath's concentration and motivation. One highlight came when she was invited to give a talk on her donkeys at school in assembly, something her teacher never thought she would have the confidence to do.

When Kath was sixteen, in the middle of her GCSE exams, Annie fell seriously ill. It had been coming on for some time, but the vet needed to operate to alleviate the suffering. Much to everyone's distress and causing severe difficulties with the school authorities, Kath would not go to school. While Annie was ill, she had to be at the stables. She said there was no point being at school as she could not concentrate, and the exams didn't matter because she knew what she wanted to do when she left.

Kath never re-took her exams. She was given full employment at the sanctuary and became one of the major contributors to its success. However, Annie had to go on red alert as Kath was a very attractive teenager and found herself a boyfriend! Annie prepared herself for seeing a lot less of her friend, but as Kath kept telling her, "I don't know what you are worrying about, he's got no chance against you." Maybe, but Annie hoped one day to be bathed, brushed and looking her best to become the number one guest at a very special wedding!

Chapter 17

Jacko

His personal handlebars

Mrs O'Leary was an elderly Irish woman with a great personality. She was nearly eighty-five and determined not to give in, even though the wet Irish climate was taking its toll with her arthritis. Even in her advanced years, Mrs O'Leary knitted for Ireland. She could knock up a wonderful sweater in two days and if ever you were lucky enough to buy one of her colourful masterpieces, you could be assured it was going to last for life.

Home was a battered old caravan parked by a hedge near West Port. Next to the van was her knitting parlour, a small garden shed full of wool, needles, patterns as well as jumpers, socks, pullovers, gloves and woolly hats of all descriptions. In the middle of all the turmoil, was her chair. It must have been at least fifty years old with well-worn woollen cushions to bolster up the occupant and keep her comfortable.

In a field next to this one-woman industrial powerhouse, lived Mrs O'Leary's other half – Jacko, a very large handsome brown donkey. Their estate of caravan, shed and field was enclosed by an electric fence for the protection of them both. The two had now been together for nearly forty years and knew each other so well. Naturally, Jacko had a knitted coat for every day of the week, he also had leg warmers, scarves and for really cold days, his earmuffs.

When Jacko had first entered Mrs O'Leary's life, she had been quick to notice the obvious; that there was something wrong with his ears. Due to mistreatment in the past, the muscles that should have held his ears up – didn't! The vet assumed it was because he had been frequently hit around the head and ears which was proven by the scars still in existence for all to see. This was all a bit sad as the donkey had the most magnificent ears, huge and covered in long hair, it was a shame to see him standing in the field with his ears at half-mast. Mrs O'Leary called them, "his personal handlebars." Jacko needed the electric fence, as Mrs O'Leary had never got around to having him gelded, so he was, as she would announce proudly in her strong Irish brogue, "Entire." This was something she was proud of, but she was also sensible enough to know that she had to take precautions if she didn't want the whole neighbourhood covered in foals, all probably recognisable, with handlebar ears!

The arthritis meant Mrs O'Leary spent nearly all her time in her chair, letting the needles do the talking. She was such a fast knitter (winner for the past thirty-two years, of the title, fastest knitter in town), she was invincible. Jacko lived a happy life. It was basic, but all his needs were met. He always had clean water and his hay nets, hanging on the shed wall, were full to the brim. He got lots of attention from visitors and friends so he was contented but it was becoming a race against time; would he or Mrs O'Leary last the longest?

The average age of a donkey is thirty-five and he was now into his early forties while Mrs O'Leary was pushing the boundaries at eighty-five, especially as she had no family for support. Finally, the cold and damp beat Mrs O'Leary. She was taken to the local hospital with pneumonia and after two weeks, she passed away. She was a well-known character in the area but had lived on her own for so long that the hospital didn't have a next of kin to notify and therefore, few knew she had died.

The field around the caravan became overgrown. Nobody thought about the one living thing that Mrs O'Leary loved the most. The hay nets were empty, the water was stagnant, and the poisonous ragwort was growing and there he was, still wondering what had happened and why his world had fallen apart. Eventually, from a nearby hotel came a wedding party, walking off the effects of the night before and they saw Jacko standing forlorn behind the hedge, wet through, his coat all matted and with his ears at half-mast, he looked a very sad donkey.

One of the wedding party was a lighting designer in a West End theatre and had heard of the Actors' Donkey Sanctuary, so after several frantic phone calls, he made it possible for Jacko to be collected and moved to England where he spent another eight glorious years with friends and children. There is a bonus to this story. In return for the kindness shown by those who rescued him, they all had their choice of beautiful pullovers, hand knitted by a very special lady and Jacko would have been very proud!

The boy that Jack built

Jacko's life had revolved around his ears. The size of them took everybody by surprise, even as a foal he had adult ears. From a few months old, they just seem to grow onwards and upwards until they reached a record size. It was because of his unique attributes that he became the most photographed donkey in the UK. Because of their size and the fact that he had been hit around the ears until he lost the muscle power to get them higher than level with his forehead, this gave them a handlebar effect. This is what made the wildlife photographers and painters bring him to life in so many of their works.

Because of the beatings, Jacko had lost his hearing. We tried several basic tests like banging a tray on the wall behind him; shouting commands which he took no notice of (well, we like to think he didn't hear them). So, Jacko was pronounced stone deaf. To most people, this would be a devastating blow but Jacko's disability was put to good use and he went on to work with children with hyper-activity and Tourette's syndrome.

He was brilliant with kids who would just spend hour after hour talking too loudly, screaming, stammering, yelling all the things that made our patience rattle and shudder. All this noise just floated past him and he carried on as if everything was dandy. At last, we had someone who could deal with these afflictions. Whereas, we might find it difficult and stressful, Jacko would head right on in there and just be a friend.

Jimmy was nine and trouble. His parents admitted that they were at their wit's end with him. He didn't sleep, he just ran up and down stairs all night, so nobody else slept either! He had no sense of fear and would take huge risks jumping off walls or play equipment. He couldn't speak at a normal level, everything had to be shouted out. He could literally deafen you during a session with him. He seemed to have no volume control. His parents desperately needed some respite and just a day away now and again would be great.

The sanctuary said we would try and help, hoping that Jacko was going to be the answer to everyone dreams. Unfortunately, at first, it didn't quite work out that way. "Jacko therapy" was very laid back. This lovely, friendly donkey would just stand and let the children run around him, stroke him, brush him and talk right in his face.

The plan was to let the child wear himself out completely. But Jacko had met his match in Jimmy. The boy never seemed to slow down even after six hours of non-stop activity. His energy level was exactly the same as when he arrived, it was uncanny! Eventually, after several sessions, even Jacko had had enough. He finally let rip and did something completely out of character, he pushed him over, not hard but enough to let Jimmy know he meant it! We were really worried about reporting to the parents why the animal had let fly. On the contrary, a week later the father came to us and said this donkey warning had had an effect of sorts. Jimmy was still terribly noisy, but he had slowed down and he was more cautious, especially when he was in Jacko's company.

At this point, I would like to be absolutely clear that at no time did Jacko ever hurt Jimmy That never happened but over the next few weeks, Jimmy did receive a few warning shoves, which made him think and slowly, the job started to get done. Jimmy started to try and please Jacko rather than having to watch out. He would not run around him completely out of control. He spent much more time at the front of the animal and he also tried to make friends with the donkey by asking his parents to buy polo mints that he could feed to Jacko. He was taught to brush him down slowly and properly. He asked if he could have a photograph to show his friends at school, which was duly given to him and his mum and dad sponsored Jacko in his name and Jimmy treasured that certificate.

The voice remained loud but there was now a distinctive mellowing of attitude. Jimmy no longer wanted to kick the stable doors in and to his mother's delight, he no longer ran up and down the stairs all night, just part of the evening before finally going to bed! Jimmy's parents affirmed to us that Jacko deserved a medal, purely for the hours of patience and persistence he put into that child's problems. Jacko passed away at forty-eight years old and Jimmy's card was the biggest on his stable door. Jimmy had hand-painted it, something the boy would never have done years earlier. He would never have been able to concentrate for long enough to complete a picture but this one he did, ears and all!

Chapter 18

Rosie and Bobbin

The surrogate mother

Rosie lived and worked on a small holding in Burnham-on-Sea, in Essex. It was a small family business consisting of a garden, nursery and a vegetable farm shop. Rosie had many varied jobs. She had a cart in which she collected the plants from the fields and delivered them to the greenhouses. She also collected the vegetables for sale in the shop. Rosie was used for a bit of ploughing and she was contented working at her own pace and enjoyed being busy.

Nothing was too strenuous, so life was very acceptable, and she was very much a part of the family. After three years of exceptionally good crops, thanks mainly to an unusually good weather pattern, the family found themselves in the position to invest and expand. More buildings were installed, and a brand-new tractor was bought. The mechanisation was welcomed by the family, but it left poor Rosie with little to do. All her tasks had been taken away from her and instead of letting her retire and graze in a field, it was decided to sell her.

Rosie was sold to a family who were about to move from Basildon to Penrith. They had plans for their retirement, starting with a new life in Cumbria. Rosie was what the wife had always wanted, so off she went. Life was good, nothing was expected of Rosie, she had a lovely paddock and the couple bought a Shetland pony to keep her company - even though she would have preferred another donkey.

Everything was fine, until the day the husband suffered a heart attack and passed away. His widow didn't drive and out in the hills, it was impossible for her to get about, so she moved into Penrith town. Once again, Rosie and the Shetland found themselves going to auction. Rosie sadly, was bought by a well-known and extremely unpleasant trader in Marple, Cheshire, one which the sanctuary had had many dealings with and had rescued several donkeys from. Rosie was kept at his yard in a broken-down railway carriage that served as stables, along with other poor creatures, all being made available for sale. On one of our regular visits to see what was going on, we noticed Rosie dejected, dirty, unhappy and coughing! The sanctuary made a rare exception and bought her and brought her back to spend the rest of her life with us.

Bobbin was quite a different story. His mother, Sable was flown into Macclesfield market from Denver, Colorado for sale. She was heavily pregnant and in an extremely bad condition from the journey. Again, the sanctuary stepped in and we got the HSBC to buy her and sponsor her. Little did we know that Sable was in fact a very valuable animal - a Sicilian Black Nose miniature.

Within a month, Sable gave birth to Bobbin. It was obviously her first foal and she had no idea what to do. She wouldn't let the poor foal anywhere near her! We found ourselves, for the first time, having to milk a donkey, not an easy task but an essential one, as Bobbin would not survive the first twenty-four hours without his mother's special milk. We were able to collect quite a substantial amount and we fed Bobbin by bottle for some time.

During this period, Rosie took a great interest in our endeavours and became like a foster mother to Bobbin. She mothered him and played with him and slept close by him at nights, as Sable was still having nothing to do with him. Bobbin was a very handsome miniature. He was very playful, and he thought that Rosie was indeed, his real mum. They bonded well and Bobbin grew up with Rosie's full attention and affection.

Sable, on the other hand found another miniature to befriend and treated Popcorn as her foal, nurturing and protecting him through his infancy, strange when she didn't want to look after her own baby. Life can unveil surprising things, but Rosie was the best thing that could have happened to Bobbin and they were very much a team, strong double act, hard to follow!

Simon's show

When we founded the Actors' Donkey Sanctuary, we decided that the charity would heavily rely on the fundraising work of the supporting actors, to keep the farm going. We wanted all children with special needs to be able to come and visit and receive therapeutic days, free of charge. We wanted to give parents of children respite and for them to be able to have quality time away from the everyday worries, work and demands made on them. We wanted every child to have access, whatever their circumstances and finally we wanted to be able to use our skills and our profession to entertain and take children on a journey that would be different and special. We wanted to give a child with special needs who has always had to rely on others for everyday tasks, a chance to care for a friend of their own; to transfer from their situation of being kept, to keeping an animal happy and sound.

The catalyst for establishing the sanctuary was a young man who found himself in extremely difficult circumstances. He was headline news in the Daily Express. Simon Bostock was nine years old, when his mother had committed suicide, unable to cope with the family's situation. Simon's father was suffering from an advanced and aggressive cancer and Simon himself, had leukaemia and was in desperate need of a bone marrow transplant. Simon's father tried desperately to help and care for his son, before he lost his own life. It was a harrowing case and one which touched the nation. To see Simon at his mother's funeral, standing by his father, who only had months to live, made us all feel inadequate. What could we do to help? Ordinary fundraising would not be quick enough to deal with this emergency. Something had to be done, fast.

As a producer, I was used to presenting shows and concerts and it was suggested that we produce an evening for Simon at The Theatre Royal, Drury Lane in London. I was surrounded by actors of great quality and fame and we started to get it together. Our aim was to present *A Night of a Hundred Stars*. Artists from all aspects of the business came forward but what we didn't expect was the lengths some of the artists would go to in helping with this project.

We had just two weeks before the show, with an audience of three thousand and possible sponsors from all over the world.

The first people to come forward were the Royal Ballet, who wanted to give a performance from their current production. Famous groups approached us to appear, as well as singers, comedians and speciality acts. One of the most rewarding things was the effort which some of the artists went to. This was especially the case with the country's leading female impersonator who travelled all the way down from Scarborough, where he was starring in his summer show. He brought with him his orchestra, dancers and singers, all at his own cost. He also insisted on getting Simon something special for himself, so he went to Hamleys toy shop and bought Simon the biggest train set we had ever seen. When Simon went backstage after the show, he saw this larger-than-life woman sitting in front of her dressing room mirror with huge eyelashes and heavy make-up. After the initial shock, he sat down, and they had a good chat.

One of the big hits of the show was our donkey Baz, who performed beautifully on stage in a sketch and Simon was desperate to meet the donkey in the flesh. He loved his time with Baz and just stroked him from head to hoof. Simon's father said he had never seen the boy with such a big smile on his face. The concert was so successful that it raised enough money for Simon's care and for him to travel with his father for a desperately needed holiday together in Malta. The legacy is the Simon Bostock Bone Marrow unit at Great Ormond Street Hospital. It gave us all confidence to open the Actors' Donkey Sanctuary and we have been able to brighten the lives of hundreds of children like Simon over the time we have been in operation.

Simon's father died on the day we rescued two donkeys from cruelty near Great Yarmouth in Norfolk. It made the day doubly sad and our thoughts went out to Simon who was now without a family.

Simon beat the leukaemia and over the years, spent many

happy times with us at the sanctuary. We were always reminded of him by Rosie and Bobbin, both very energetic donkeys who loved music, so they became the emblem for another concert at Drury Lane, which we called *To Tina with Love,* presented to help down's syndrome.

Tina had down's syndrome and therefore, had to have many operations to repair her heart. She was, in our estimation, one of the bravest youngsters we had ever known. As soon as one operation was completed, then another, it seemed, had to follow soon afterwards. It was as if she spent her entire childhood in the operating theatre and was incredibly brave. On a few occasions, her favourite donkey, Bobbin was allowed to visit her in hospital in Manchester. Bobbin would only travel with Rosie, so the two of them had to be covered in green theatre sheets and wait in the hospital car park while Tina came down in a wheelchair to see them.

Rosie and Bobbin were known as the dancing donkeys because of their choreographic moves and Tina herself was a huge dance fan and wanted very much to attend dance classes when she got better and was able to do so. In total, Tina underwent seventeen operations and thankfully, afterwards, was able to live comfortably and contentedly. She visited the donkeys on a regular basis. They both loved their Zumba classes which took place now and again in the donkeys' big barn. All three of them threw themselves into it wholeheartedly and we could never work out who was more tired at the end of it but there was one thing for sure, they all three loved it and that made it all worthwhile!

Chapter 19

Pepsi

Getting away from everything

At a small French village, six miles from La Rochelle, there was a farmhouse with twenty acres of arable land and a paddock on which two brown donkeys grazed. One was a mare, called Cerise and the other, a gelding called Pepsi. The area was a quaint and viable tourist trap, out of the way, typically French and untouched by the hustle and bustle of normal everyday life. In the village square, the locals gathered morning and evening for their croque-monsieur. With their news and views of the day's events, much bread was broken, and many daily problems solved or at least corrected.

Cerise and Pepsi were very much a part of village life, respected for their work which although hard, they both found very enjoyable. This work consisted of taking couples for a week's trek around the beautiful French countryside in small but compact wooden caravans which had just enough room to sleep in, with camping equipment to cook on, when no French cafés were available. The holidays were idyllic, especially if you liked getting away from everything: a lovely little Romany caravan pulled by a lovely brown donkey, stop where you liked, when you liked, and the only requirement was that you looked after the animal properly. You had to treat them with care and follow the regulations for their meals, their grooming and their general well-being; so, no great hardship there. The donkeys loved their work and participated in all aspects of the holiday, making for even fonder memories. The pair of them appeared in more holiday photo albums than anyone else.

After breakfast for the caravanners and a bucket for Pepsi, the first morning's walk was about five miles or six kilometres at a very gentle pace, enjoying the scenery and peace. Lunch was leisurely with bread, cheese and maybe wine; then off for another five kilometres, finishing at teatime, and so it went on for six quiet days. The holiday makers' only problems came when they have to say goodbye to their companion donkey; tears were often shed. The donkeys received cards from all over the world as their efforts and friendship were obviously well appreciated.

We had no idea how old Pepsi was when Cerise died aged thirty, but Pepsi went into a steep decline. He had lived all his life with his beloved mother, and they had shared everything together. Pepsi was grieving. He would stand alone by his water trough for days, he wouldn't eat, nor would he go into his shelter, whatever the weather. To make matters worse, his owner had developed multiple sclerosis and was finding life very difficult, having to adjust from a very active life!

There was no way Pepsi was fit enough to take customers out on a week's holiday but there was one journey the owner thought he might still like to do. An elderly actress used to holiday there every year and they all got on famously. For the lady, it was her annual retreat, to get away from the lights and the crowds. Even though she was in her eighties, she was still very active. She was very sorry that Cerise had gone but agreed to see how things went and she was quite prepared to stay at the farm for the week if Pepsi was unable to holiday with her.

The lady arrived on Sunday and had dinner with the family before going out to see Pepsi. He was visibly pleased to see her again, but she was quite taken aback that Pepsi had lost so much weight and was looking so alone and forlorn. On Monday morning, they went for a walk just to the village and back, they both shared a baguette with a lengthy chat and a lot of stroking. They spent two hours sitting in the village square in the sunshine, both understanding what he was going through. When they got back, instead of going to the paddock gate, Pepsi pulled her to the barn and stood by the side of his caravan ready to be harnessed and take her for a ramble in the countryside. They spent a glorious five days together quietly and very sedately plodding around, nothing planned or worked out as usual, just as it came, stopping when Pepsi wanted to stop and just relaxing together. "That was the best holiday ever," she told the owner when they got back. However, knowing the farmer was ill and he was having to sell the caravans and the business, she knew it was also her last journey.

This was too much and before she left, she asked the landlord if he would consider selling Pepsi to her, so she could take him back to the Actors' Donkey Sanctuary, where he would have other donkey friends and do such valuable work with children. So it was that Pepsi arrived at the sanctuary and spent many years accompanying me on my talks and working with hundreds of children from all over the UK. He went to schools, theatres, church halls and even a hospital. He was very popular amongst the donkeys and had many hundreds of human friends!

Talking the hind leg off a donkey

All the donkeys here at the sanctuary helped children to overcome difficulties, reach ambitions and generally improve their lives. In most cases, they were just there for the children, handing out therapeutic friendship at which they were experts. Then would come a moment when one donkey would stand out, when they bonded with someone and make an unbreakable partnership and I was fortunate enough to have that very precious association. Therefore, I take this opportunity to relate my own experience; to pay tribute to someone very special, very clever, intelligent, extremely kind and patient - and he needed to be.

Pepsi was my donkey and together we worked and travelled hundreds of miles. I worked in theatre so was used to being on the road but for Pepsi, it was a totally new way of life but one which he took to so fast and so easily. On our travels, he got many nicknames. People would call him, "My after-dinner donkey," even "My after-eight mint." When I was booked to do a talk, they would say, "You will bring that incredible donkey with you. My wife doesn't believe what I told her about it."

When I prepared for a talk, I used to gather and sort all my huge photo cards. Some of the stories were so incredible, I found it easier to show the actual photo, as people found it hard to believe what I was telling them. Pepsi would be enjoying his tea in his stable with his wife Oxo when he would spot me putting my photos in the trailer. He would kiss the wife goodnight and bang on the stable door to let me know he was ready to be loaded. I would put his best leather head collar on and one of his woollen coats, knitted by local Women's Institutes especially for him.

Each coat was made up of fifty-two six-inch squares, all different colours and he had six coats for all seasons! I never had to lead Pepsi with a rope that just wasn't necessary; he climbed the ramp into his trailer which was a five-star hotel, with everything he needed including treats, hay nets and lighting. He loved it and it felt very much his own which is exactly what it was. Each venue was new, with very different needs and requirements. One evening, it would be a village hall, the next a school assembly hall, a theatre, a church, a hotel dining room and so on.

I had to adapt my talk accordingly but without a word of consultation, Pepsi would weigh up the scene for himself and often decided where it would be best to stand so everybody got a good view of him (ego - what ego?). He had his own floor covering - just in case of an accident! But I can say in all honesty, that in the six years we worked together, the floor cloth stayed clean. If we were in a gymnasium or on a dance floor, he would wear his specially made boots, so he didn't slip or leave a scratch.

There were moments in the talk when I needed him to react and for these moments, we did have to have fairly lengthy rehearsal periods but once it was ingrained in his brain, it stayed there for good. I would look at him after turning a photo and ask if he was ready for a polo mint. He would nod and I would ask a lady in the audience to do the honours. He would accept the polo and always nod, as if to say thank you. It took three months of daily effort to learn that trick and I got through packet after packet of mints, but he never asked for more than one from an audience. No donkey in the world would do that, normally they would have your hand off for the whole packet, but he was good.

If I asked him if he was alright, he would nod yes and at one point, I would ask him to come nearer the easel where the photos were, which he duly did. But the cleverest moment was when I reached the end of my talk (which he must have been so grateful for), he would always recognise the last photo which was all blue and he would move away from me and face the door, as if getting ready to leave. In reality, he was getting ready to meet his adoring fans. The audience would queue up at the end of the talk to stroke and have a chat with him.

I often felt that after an hour of talking and entertaining they might talk to me but I soon realised who it was they wanted to meet and we both knew they would donate money to his collection basket, which lay strategically in front of him! Sometimes, it took hours. After talks like the British Legion annual conference, three thousand women all wanted his autograph and a copy of his autobiography - that took a while. He had a special ink hoof printer which I would stamp on his books. They even asked me to endorse his latest work now and again!

Pepsi worked the London Palladium, Great Ormond Street Children's Hospital, the Savoy Hotel and prestigious venues up and down the country. He was once covered in cellophane so he could visit children in cancer wards. He visited dozens of hospices, schools, libraries, over five-hundred Women's Institutes, plus many Inner Wheels, Rotary Clubs, Lions and golf clubs. You name it, he played it. He got a telegram once from Morecambe and Wise "I bet you haven't played the Jungle Café, Shap?"

When Pepsi passed away at the age of forty-one, I gave up the talks. I just couldn't go on stage without him, it was too painful. I always appreciated how well-known double acts felt when one left. There is never a way to recapture those moments and it's best not to try. Pepsi raised thousands of pounds over his career and it is doubtful if the sanctuary would ever have got on a firm footing financially without him and I can assure you, never a day goes by that I don't smile when I think of him.

Chapter 20

Diva

Abandoned outside a *Little Chef*

Portsmouth in Hampshire and a call for help was made from the cattery in nearby Gosport. An actress had been to open the annual open day celebrations at this astonishing charity, which rescued cats from all over the country. It had an amazing setting as when you entered the home. You walked down a cobbled street of fascinating terraced houses reminiscent of Coronation Street itself (which we understood it was modelled on). All the windows had nets and ornaments, all the doors were painted different colours, with letter boxes and door knockers and the names of the inhabitants on the walls outside. The only difference was the whole street was inhabited by over two hundred cats, all rescued and all happily living together in this surreal setting. The actress has helped the charity for some time but what was concerning her this morning, was an incident she witnessed on her journey down.

Two mules have been abandoned at the *Little Chef* on the Winchester bypass and as all animal charities work together against cruelty, the actress knew the cattery would help if they could. Two helpers from the charity went with her and they headed back to the *Little Chef*. They found the two mules, one a red coloured mare, the other was larger and dark brown. Both were distraught and traumatised by all the noisy traffic. They were tethered by ropes to the restaurant sign at the opening to the car park and the place was busy with drivers coming and going. The police had attempted to move the animals but had been unable to get close enough to untie the ropes. The mules were scared and hostile, which was giving cause for concern. A vet had been called for further instructions.

Both mules had extensive injuries, marks of severe cruelty leaving scars and scabs all over them and some wounds were new and in need of attention. The vet was able to sedate both animals to have a closer look and determined that indeed, they had both suffered quite considerably from harsh and cruel treatment. A trailer was called for and the mules were carefully coaxed into the vehicle in a state of stupor. The mules were dealt with, cleaned up and moved to a safe location near Oxford where they were housed with twelve donkeys, who had themselves been rescued.

After a month, the mules were much better and in their final report, the vet suggested that the company of the donkeys had done more for their recovery than any medication. Unfortunately, the small donkey site in Oxford was full and they asked if the mules could be moved to the Actors' Donkey Sanctuary. This is where we came in and the animals, Marmite and Diva, went on to spend twenty-one happy years with us.

The female mule was a real Diva. Not only was she sponsored by one of this country's biggest opera stars, but she also had an actors' fan club as her main sponsor. The actor in question had been a star for many years. His voice had that certain quality that made women's toes turn up and he had always been blessed with extremely good looks. Even in his sixties, he was immensely fanciable to women of all ages. He rescued many donkeys and brought them to the sanctuary. His army of lady fans had discovered this and saw this as their way into his company.

The fan club was run by a very attractive lady called Michelle and fortunately for us, she was a little more reserved and sedate than the majority of club members. Diva was a difficult mule and for that reason, she could not work with children. Also, she was not good with the general public. She was never been able to trust people again and kept herself very much to herself. Enter Michelle and Diva took to her immediately and for no apparent reason other than there was an instant liking. Michelle agreed to take on this awkward mule to see if she could help. After a few weeks of visiting regularly, the mule took to her in a big way. They went for walks together, she allowed Michelle to brush her, even wash her and they sat and chatted for hours in the side meadow.

The successful work with the mule, partially put Michelle's

urgent need to meet her actor on hold but it wasn't long before the fan club heard of her successful infiltration into his charity and plans were set up to manoeuvre into the charity on the pretence of animal welfare. As a fund-raising event, our heart throb actor had arranged an open day at which he would appear (which was a very infrequent occurrence). Money was desperately needed to keep the donkeys' home and the children's therapy going, so he wrote an article in the charity's seasonal newsletter to ask for help with his latest quest to raise enough to keep the place going. The response was unbelievable. Michelle arrived a week after the announcement with a cheque for two thousand pounds, having jumped out of an aeroplane at several thousand feet into a boggy field. Another lady fan had driven a motor bike around the wall of death in a fun fair in London. Three women had done a bungee jump from a frightening height and sent him cheques to the value of many hundreds of pounds. They baked, they cycled, they rowed, they ran, they held Zumba classes! What brilliant ladies – and in the end, they raised a phenomenal sum for their hero's open day.

Although there was method in their madness and they got to spend an afternoon with him, it was heart-warming for us to see that they were genuinely glad they had made such an effort, both for the children and the animals. They looked upon the actor with different eyes, an ordinary man who cared desperately for animals. In return, he responded well to their good wishes, accepting the flattery but, at the same time, being able to convey his gratitude for their mammoth efforts. Everybody was a winner. Diva, of course, couldn't care less. She only wanted to be assured that Michelle would be back soon with more polos.

Not one bray goes by

Our two mules settled in well after their traumatic experiences, but it was a learning curve for us as well. We had never had mules before and knew very little about them. However, it was evident straightaway, that they were very different from donkeys, although their lineage was also well mixed. The first thing we noticed was that they didn't get on together, they did not want to share a box and when we put them together, there were quite fearsome battles, especially instigated by the mare.

It was something we couldn't work out until we contacted the British Mule Association who put us in the picture. Apparently, the male mule has no reproductive genes, so cannot sire any foals. The mare has to be served by a donkey or a horse to conceive a foal. So, knowing the mule is of no use to her, she subjects him to humiliating and rather upsetting abuse. Rather than allow this to go on, we separated the pair at night. We then had to find partners for them both, which wasn't as hard as it sounds as they were both spending their days out in the meadows with over fifty donkeys and they made the choice themselves.

The male mule, Marmite met his friend on a bright summer's day, when a very pretty Shetland came to stay while one of our patrons went on holiday for six weeks. She was Dixie, a middle-aged pony whose home was with a family in Bournemouth. Her life was also going to change because it was love at first sight and they moved into together rather sooner than anticipated. One evening, not long after her arrival, Marmite followed Dixie into her stable and it was evident that they were destined for each other, but we kept wondering what would happen when the six weeks were up?

We decided to contact the actor and spoil his holiday, but as luck would have it, he was going to approach us to ask that if the pony did well, would we give her a home? As his children were now too big to ride her. What luck!

They spent nineteen years happily together until Dixie died just after her thirtieth birthday. Once again, we were to learn something about mules. Marmite was so distressed by her death that he grieved for a year! We couldn't get him to eat properly and he just refused to join the others. He spent the whole time alone in his corner of the meadow where he and Dixie had spent so many happy times. He just couldn't and wouldn't get over it until, Diva his fellow mule took pity on him and went to keep him company. It was a slow process, but she persevered and after months of patient nagging, she won him over and they became a couple again after all those years.

After she came to the attention of a famous opera singer, we named our female mule Diva, which actually suited her admirably. The singer kindly undertook concerts on Diva's behalf, singing in the Sheffield Concert Hall with the Black Dyke Mills Band which brought much needed funds to the sanctuary.

The major problem for us was that the mules could not do any work with children, not because they were naturally nervous but because they could not forget the past and the scars of their youth. They were unapproachable, but they roamed around the meadows freely and never ever harmed or made any visitors feel uncomfortable, they just kept themselves to themselves, except for one glorious occasion.

The Actors' Donkey Sanctuary was close to a village called Darley Dale and in that pretty little place was a special care home for the elderly. It was special because there were some very important inhabitants whose lives were going to change owing to the efforts and care of our two mules. Four men in their eighties lived in the home. They had very vivid and courageous memories from World War Two. Enter the mules, at last, their work could start.

The men had been part of the forgotten army which had fought in Burma and two had fought valiantly through the jungle with their beloved mules by their side. All four had been Japanese prisoners of war, working on the infamous railway. Norman related how his mule had to pull a gun carriage for days through heavy terrain, a feat of strength unimaginable to us. They slept with their mules for warmth in the cold nights. They even fed the mules with anything they could find before feeding themselves, such was their reliance on the animals' strength.

When a mule died, it was catastrophic, and a great sadness went right through the company.

There were twenty-eight mules with the regiment, but they lost nineteen during the conflict. Had they not had their mules, not one soldier would have got through alive. One can only imagine how they felt when we took Marmite and Diva to the home to meet the boys. To see grown men cry openly at the arrival of these two animals said it all. We wondered whether we had done the right thing bringing them but after an hour in the animals' presence, we realised that it was a good move and one that lasted until all four men were gone.

The story doesn't end there. David and Norman had re-membered our mules in their wills which was in itself a very emotional moment for us. Diva then had Dave's Burma Star on her door, with a special framed message to commemorate all mules everywhere and Marmite had Norman's Army beret on his door. We really treasured them. In the end, the mules came good and gave back some happiness, bringing back memories which the men never thought they would be able to relive together and especially not with mules by their side.

Chapter 21

Kojak

More than a handful

Uttoxeter. The focus of attention this early morning was a very big donkey, trying forcefully to escape the traders who had brought him in. They were no match for his strength and had to seek stewards' assistance to try and lead him into a sales pen. The noticeable scars on his back and head, limping on his back leg were an indication that he has been ill-treated and was fighting back. His head collar was so tight around his head that one eye was very swollen. As he was a stallion, he had to be penned alone as there were several donkeys and mares around in the pens and his senses were playing havoc with him. He was a very majestic beast with big ears and a white blaze across his forehead. One could only imagine what the rest of him was like with the matted coat covered in lice with maggots under each of his shoulder blades. His feet had not been attended to for some months, probably even years. The consequences had left him with twisted hooves and long horns making it difficult to walk and throwing the legs out of sync. It was debatable whether the market should, in fact, have put this animal up for sale at all and the market inspector was sent for to give his opinion. The decision was quickly made to let the animal go through to auction basically bypassing the animal welfare side of things and trying to get rid of him as fast as possible!

Attempting to tie him to a ring proved both impossible and dangerous to the handlers, so he was left free in his pen which didn't take him long to demolish. He was moved to a brick stable normally used for working horses. It took four men to guide him along the row of pens to the end stables where he was released. He circled endlessly around and around, scraping the ground, braying extremely loudly making all the other animals restless and nervous. The mares at one end of the barn answered his repeated calls with their own bray which momentarily made him stop and listen.

The schedule for the day's auction was being revised quickly to get this animal through first and away. The stewards were convening in one corner of the auction room debating which of them was going to risk life and limb to get this donkey into the ring and march him round for viewing. The decision was put to the auctioneer that it was too dangerous to bring him in and he should be seen in his stable by those who wished to purchase. The auctioneer considered he was too disruptive and would make all the animals difficult to show correctly. So, they ordered him to be removed from the sale.

The owners refused to take him back as they had had enough trouble getting him there and they were obviously not prepared to waste any more time with him. They were prepared to forego the price and they listed him for the slaughter men to take him for the meat market.

Meanwhile, in the stable block, a lady made an offer for him and it was accepted. She had a horsebox in the car park, and she offered money to anyone who would help her load him up. Money talks and at the sight of pound notes, men come out of the woodwork to assist. Even the stewards, who were not prepared to take him round the ring, suddenly had a change of heart, as they sensed financial remuneration for their efforts. Within five minutes, there were at least twenty men hanging around the donkey waiting to bring him out. They circled around him and he had the largest escort ever seen all the way to the horsebox. After sums of money were distributed amongst the crowd of helpers, the ramp was lifted, and the donkey was ready for a short journey to Ashbourne in Derbyshire.

Arriving at Ashbourne, the donkey was released into a five-acre field and tried to run around and stretch his tired and uncomfortable limbs. Rolling in the mud indicated that he was beginning to relax a little. Over the period of three weeks, the owner did all she could to get Kojak, as she has named him, right. The decision was made to castrate him, as this would make him calmer, able to join other animals and in the long run, have a better more sociable existence. His age was a problem as aged donkeys do find the recovery period harder than the foals, who are just straight back on their feet and away bouncing and playing within hours of the operation. Kojak at twenty-two, found it more difficult. He bled a lot and spent a few days recovering in his stable.

Having now got Kojak back to full health, the lady wanted him to go somewhere where he would be useful, well cared for and where she could visit him from time to time. She approached the Actors' Donkey Sanctuary which was just eight miles away and asked if they would home her donkey. They accepted and were very grateful for both what she had done for the animal and extremely thankful for her generosity towards the charity.

Brick by brick

A phone call requesting an unusual possibility was made to the sanctuary from a house of correction in Wigan. Would it be possible for us to accommodate six young offenders between the ages of sixteen and eighteen and their instructor to do some charitable work as part of their hopeful relocation into society. The course chosen was bricklaying and the aim of the exercise was that the youngsters would repair and rebuild sections of the sanctuary that needed repair and build new walls where necessary. There would be five boys and one girl, and the instructor would be there at all times to give tuition and to make sure all was well. It would have to be a residency, as there was no means of transporting the youngsters to the sanctuary and back each day. This gave us food for thought, as that meant that they would have to live with us in the farmhouse and we were not convinced this would be possible or even safe, as the youngsters had rather serious crimes against them. It was, however, decided that we should attempt it.

The first problem that arose was that the girl had to stay under the same roof as the boys and it appeared after the first night that she would have to be somewhat guarded as the boys would not leave her alone! Having been vetted by three different people as to whether we would be a suitable establishment to care for these youngsters, we were disappointed to realise that the man they had actually sent to instruct and supervise was totally useless. He just put on his slippers at seven, lit his pipe, turned on the television and let the youngsters do anything they wanted without any care for the consequences or the environment!

The boys were out of control and the sanctuary was of little interest to them except for the daily attempt to break into the collection boxes and the shop till. The girl was a very different kettle of fish and spent many hours of her free time getting acquainted with the donkeys, especially Kojak, who she had an obvious liking for.

While they were building their walls, unsupervised, as the instructor had now gone off for walks and shopping sprees in neighbouring villages, Kojak would start to come over and spend time with his new friend, showing her some sort of encouragement and enthusiasm for what she was trying to do. The boys had no interest in the donkeys except seeing who could target one with a missile, but the young girl was showing signs of success both with her job and with the animals.

The girl had been abused in earlier times, both physically and sexually, by her father. She had run away from home at twelve and been shunted around care homes for two or three years. She took to crime as a means of survival, trying to get money to have things that others had but she was caught every time. She had not had any meaningful relationship with adults or boys, and she was finding it difficult to accept the advances the boys were dishing out.

Of all the people around her, Kojak was the only person she trusted. That was something he could build on. Slowly, Kojak stayed with her through all the work periods, never moving away until she had finished her tasks. He would stand beside her and make a divide between her and the boys. If they started messing about, he stood his ground very firmly confirming whose side he was on. Now, in the evenings, they would spend time together in his stable and she asked if she could spend the nights with him as she had a camp bed. It was an unusual request but if one young offender got something out of this trip, it was deemed a success, so they spent the nights together. It also became noticeable that the boys left her alone more and the teasing and the bullying stopped, as she turned her way of life around. It was also noticed that her work was by far the best and the boys had wasted their time.

Kojak got his stable walls repaired. He even got a small field shelter built where he could take refuge from the weather. We were keen to photograph her work and to make sure that the authorities were made aware of her efforts and her building prowess, as the instructor had no idea of what she had achieved, nor did he care!

The five boys went back to their offenders' home and were soon back to their old ways and in trouble within a week of their return. "Our girl" was sent out into the world on license and immediately started to forge forward in an attempt to better herself and regain her dignity and show what lay under all the troubled exterior that life had bought her way.

The young lady married two years later to a very kind and safe young man and having been a volunteer at the sanctuary for over seven years, she brought her own daughter Lilly to come and meet her devoted friend and companion. Kojak gave Lilly the donkey treatment that made her mother's life turn around. "Her Knight in shining armour," is how she described Kojak. Couldn't put it better ourselves.

Chapter 22

Columbine

Beware the picnic snatcher

Columbine was born in a small fishing village in southern France called Guethary, flanked by two seaside resorts - Saint Jean de Luz and Biarritz, both immensely busy towns especially in the summer months owing to the very long sandy beaches. They were a great favourite with the French themselves close to the Spanish border and the town of Saint Sebastien.

As life became more commercial and shops sprang up along the small village market street, the local flavour was evaporating, replaced with bars and gift outlets to accommodate the new and younger intake of visitors. There were still remnants of the old way of life. Just a mile up in the hills and along the coastal paths, old French farm buildings were still clinging on to fading peasant traditions. One of those family traditions was the ownership of a donkey. Most French farms believed rigorously that to have a donkey on the farm was lucky. Even when the tractors came, the farmers were reluctant to get rid of their donkeys. This meant that the animal was of no use, except keeping the superstition alive, so they were discarded to a part of the land which was of no use and left to fend for themselves.

Columbine was very fortunate, as her farm ran alongside a very popular cliff walk which joined Guethary to Saint Jean de Luz. It was used by walkers, both local and tourist, so she developed certain methods by which she could attract passing trade and relieve them of their picnics and food. During the hot months, on a good day, she would manage sandwiches and fruit doughnuts from the catering van along the way. Strawberries were a favourite but the best of all, were the ice creams which she somehow managed to steal. She became so adept at relieving passers-by of their entire picnics, that complaints began arriving at the local mayor's office. Putting the matter in perspective, if no-one fed her, she would have to fend for herself and as Columbine would tell you, seven months in the winter were pretty tough and lonely!

Two actors had bought a holiday home in the village and would walk past Columbine's sad looking face - they soon realised she was destitute. They learnt from the farmer that she was going to have to go to the market as he was getting too many complaints and he didn't have the funds to keep her indoors. He was going to what the French romantically call, the 'Horse Market', which in reality is a meat market. Columbine was destined to become salami on a French menu! The actors couldn't stand the thought and as they had no land with their French home, they decided to take her home with them and hope that the Actors' Donkey Sanctuary would help with homing her.

Columbine was able to travel on a ferry across the Bay of Biscay to Portsmouth, then by road to Derbyshire and on to the sanctuary. She settled in well, except for her old habit of frisking visitors of their picnics! The sanctuary had just built a new picnic area with a magnificent view of the Derbyshire Dales. The public could sit in these blissful surroundings with cream teas, admiring the views and of course, the donkeys who would line up for attention, except for Columbine, who would line up for something completely different.

She had now savoured Derbyshire cream teas and was partial, if not obsessed, with getting hold of them. She had devised means of distraction which made the herd go the opposite way while she targeted the unsuspecting victims. She had to act fast when she had homed in on the food, which she nearly always got with great success. The tea rooms could not cater for the extra demand from those who had literally lost their cream teas.

The vet happened to make a remark which brought the problem to our attention. "Without an examination, is that donkey pregnant?" he asked. Columbine had overdone the pilfering and her pirate activities were brought to a sudden and drastic halt. She was boxed for two weeks to get some weight off and then introduced to her very own private paddock which was far away from temptation. She became slimmer but there was still that look on her face when she saw visitors, that suggested it wouldn't take much for her to get straight back into her old habits.

Heart-to-heart

In the Hallamshire Hospital, Sheffield, the cardiac and stroke unit were awaiting an urgent case of a young child having suffered a suspected heart attack at school. The teacher's response had been professional, and the paramedics had responded quickly and efficiently with treatment on the scene. Samantha was ten years old with no previous medical history. To all intents and purposes a healthy child, good at sports, able twice weekly, to swim four lengths of her local swimming pool. Her parents arrived with the ambulance and were quite naturally, distraught and extremely anxious at the scene in front of them. The doctors were able to confirm that she had, in fact, experienced a heart attack and monitored the situation as she was taken to the intensive care unit. The prompt action of everyone concerned had given Samantha a fighting chance.

All the medical evidence pointed to a problem with a valve and this was dealt with surgically. It was also found that the effects of the sizeable heart attack had left Samantha with temporary loss of the use of her left leg and arm, but her speech had not been impaired which was considered a positive thing. Now, the emphasis was on rest, monitoring in intensive care and waiting. The parents shared a schedule of being with her and were given a relation's room in case any further or sudden matters arose.

Progress was made in the first few days and Samantha gathered strength. She was able to communicate with her parents and the hospital staff but unable to move. It was suggested that a course of physiotherapy be initiated to assist her to regain some movement, if at all possible.

A week had gone by and the first physiotherapy had been completed with little effect but as they explained, it was very early stages. Samantha's had been a surprisingly rare and unexpected case of heart failure for one so young and so her room was never short of medical students seeking to gain knowledge first-hand!

At the Lyceum Theatre, Sheffield, a musical was in full swing and the star of the show was browsing through the local paper basically to see if she had received good or bad reviews for her opening night! She came across Samantha's story and the race against time to bring her back to life. Her courage motivated the artist to ask if she could visit sometime during her week's stay in the city. Samantha's parents were very receptive to the idea, as the actress was extremely well-known, and it was considered it would be of benefit to Samantha. A meeting was arranged to take place in between the Thursday matinee and the evening performance. The artist would have to come fully made up as it would be a dash back to the theatre to appear in the evening performance.

Samantha was thrilled to see the actress and they sat together for over an hour. Samantha had lots of questions about the TV shows she had seen. The actress, however, was more inclined to know what the next moves were to improve Samantha's condition. She noticed a framed photo by the side of Samantha's bed. "Who is that?" the actress asked. "That's Columbine," replied Samantha, "My adopted donkey." "That's interesting, you expect a family member or even a boyfriend but not a donkey, Columbine must be very special," the actress observed.

After talking more and having to race back to the theatre, the artist had gathered all the information she required about the donkey!

On Saturday, a cheque arrived at the Actors' Donkey Sanctuary for a thousand pounds. The actress had asked the Thursday night audience if they would join her in donating so that Samantha's donkey, Columbine, could have something from Samantha towards vet bills. She wanted to set up means for

Samantha to spend time with her best friend! It was a lovely gesture, and much appreciated by the sanctuary, especially as it was from an actress that we admired greatly and fitted so well with our mandate.

Samantha left hospital after six weeks and went home to convalesce for a month before she could attempt a journey. The visit finally came and the two were together again but then the astonishing part took place.

Samantha's physiotherapy had not been able to give back her movement in her leg and arm and she was now in a wheelchair. It was too hard to walk for more than a few yards at a time. Her actress benefactor had sent a grooming kit to Samantha so that she could brush Columbine, which they both enjoyed very much. To get around the donkey with the brush and comb was hard in the wheelchair, so Samantha made a tremendous effort and with Columbine's strong back she raised herself up and managed to hold on for dear life and brush her all over, before falling back into her chair, exhausted but fulfilled.

Over the next few months, Samantha managed more and more contact with Columbine, and it was making an obvious improvement in her physical ability. Her parents were delighted and so were her doctors, who found it interesting that the animal had acted as a go between and made such a difference to the child.

On Samantha's twelfth birthday, she was driven to Scarborough by her mum and dad, where she met up with Columbine who was waiting for her on the beach. Miraculously, the pair, accompanied by a strong support team and the actress, embarked on a walk from coast-to-coast, eventually arriving to a civic reception at Blackpool Town Hall. It had taken Samantha and Columbine three weeks and four days to complete the walk raising a substantial amount of money for the heart foundation.

It was an exceptional feat to be attempted by both of them and one which we know astounded all around who were involved with the case. Into her twenties, life was a little quieter for the Samantha, but she still visited Columbine each weekend and the bond between them just got stronger and stronger.

Chapter 23

Herbie

As good as a third-year art student

Herbie was the most loved animal by children, mainly owing to his total understanding of their needs. Herbie had an incredible mind and ability and there were many times when one had to remember that he was, indeed, a donkey. To have a conversation with Herbie was quite normal. Visitors to the sanctuary found it odd that we all talked to him for long periods of time, as if he understood every word. The truth of the matter was that he did!

Bill was ten years old when he first confronted Herbie. His lack of communication gave the donkey time for thought. The fact that the young boy was confined to his wheelchair was also a challenge in the distances they could walk together. Both Bill and Herbie had a common bond. Because the boy could not communicate, he had taken to writing and drawing in notebooks to attract people to his needs and requirements.

The doodling had turned to sketches, making records of his favourite moments. Spending many hours in the meadows, Herbie by the side of his chair, he came up with some outstanding drawings, which his carers were keen to promote. They wanted to encourage and push this natural ability which was fast turning into something very special. The main theme of his latest works was Herbie. The portraits Bill came up with were not only unbelievably realistic but also very professional. When a visiting art teacher from Stockport Art College brought a party of ladies on a day out to paint the surroundings, the donkeys were keen to put young Bill's work forward for his appraisal. The teacher was truly overwhelmed that a ten-year old with the disabilities he had, was able to conjure up such great pictures. He explained, not only the donkey but the surroundings, had been beautifully rendered and constructed in a manner of a third-year art student. He asked to meet Bill and tried to explain his feelings towards his outstanding contribution to art and what a role model he would make for those who perhaps needed that extra push to create images of their own.

Bill listened hard to every word and seemingly understood

but he stopped the teacher and pointed to Herbie and on the bottom of a drawing, he wrote, "The trouble is, not everybody has a Herbie!" The teacher smiled, perhaps not taking in the honesty behind that statement but we knew exactly what he meant.

Some of Bill's works were taken to the college and a small exhibition was mounted. Bill was invited to the opening but would only consider the invitation if it was for two, which logistically was difficult for us to organise, but we managed it and they both went. Herbie behaved perfectly and never left Bill's side. As for Bill, he was far more interested in everyone being introduced to his donkey than admiring his works!

Bill became an artist in his teens, and he has two studios: one at his home in a converted old loft, the other in the stable next to Herbie's, which he spent much more time in. Herbie's walls were always festooned with lovely colourful works and when we had open days, Bill always had a stall and raised more money than anyone else could. The combination of the two of them together was lethal in relieving visitors of their hard-earned cash.

Herbie was approached by *The Tweenies* to appear in their show. Because it was difficult to get to the studios, the crew decided to come to Herbie's home instead. Much to the delight of the children, who turned up in their hundreds to see the massive puppets. Herbie loved being the centre of attention and became a natural at playing his part in the proceedings. So successful was the whole thing that they all came back twice and did two more shows.

Being made aware of the sanctuary and its work and in total awe of Bill's paintings, *The Tweenies* offered to do a concert for children in the meadow, in a huge marquee, bringing their orchestra with them. We were totally overwhelmed by the whole proceedings. When over two thousand children piled in and had the best time of their lives, it was a real thrill. Herbie appeared at the end surrounded by *The Tweenies* to the delight of the children and he showed signs of being overwhelmed by the response given to him, although he was slightly nervous at all the clapping and whistling that went on.

Herbie and Bill were inseparable. They literally looked after each other when they were together. When Bill got to eighteen, he was given a special car fitted out with everything he needed, making him more mobile. It was now possible for him to increase his visits. When the car approached the sanctuary along the mile-long drive, Herbie would canter to the gate and wait patiently for it to come into the car park. Then a bray of welcome, as Bill got his chair out and made ready for their day together.

When Herbie passed away in his fortieth year, Bill was philosophical about the event. He kept the stable next to Herbie and kept painting but the work he turned out was not as bright or as creative as when his pal was by his side. In the end, Bill showed his grief for his lost friend and became very insular and wouldn't go out. Life was not the same and however much we tried to introduce a new friend, that effort was very firmly rejected. There was no one else as far as Bill was concerned.

All of us at the sanctuary, especially hundreds of children, missed Herbie very much. We were reminded daily through Bill's lovely caricatures and portraits of him, but we also felt a huge loss at not seeing Bill and all that he meant to us. Herbie had worked so hard to bring Bill out of himself and did such a superb job of it. We felt he would be sad to see his friend in the reclusive world he had now built around himself.

Epilogue

Remembered with much love

The next stage for us and the sanctuary

As the years passed, I continued to use my entertainment industry contacts to help create income for the sanctuary as the costs and expenses never stopped. Without the valuable and much appreciated donations and funds generated by our well-known patrons and supporters from the world of theatre, television and music, we could not have kept going.

While all of this was unfolding, age had been of little concern to me, just numbers that roll forward of little consequence. When some brave person with whom who I was well acquainted mentioned the notion of retirement, it took me by surprise. I can honestly say I had given it little thought to the subject, and it was of little interest to me. Like many of my generation, my mentality was still reflecting that of my school days, but I had to admit that physically, things were perhaps becoming a little more strenuous than I would have wished for.

Annie and I were living in an idyllic but isolated rural setting. In the summer months, we spent much time on our bench on the terrace, surrounded by beasts of burden and affectionate Cypriot terriers. However, the winter months were unavoidable. We could not get away from the strong winds, the interminable rain and the cold. Also, mucking out seventy donkeys who needed a lot of attention, plus a days' work introducing or writing were seemingly, taking their toll. Annie was running the popular tearoom, was working with children with special needs and her dressmaking and designs needed attention so, she too, was feeling the pressure of time and motion.

As we entered our seventies, I decided that not only was the time moving on, but it was possible, after twenty-nine years, that we might not be as forward thinking or modernised to cope with the vast alterations that life was throwing up at us. It made me realise that perhaps, someone younger, with new ideas would be more beneficial. However, I found it impossible to attract a responsible couple or person to take over the mantle.

Then one morning, I received a call from Judy Giles. She

was running a small but important donkey foundation, in a small village outside Truro down in Cornwall, which her mother had created some years earlier. Judy had researched all relevant donkey sanctuaries before calling me. She had chosen me as a preferred start for her questions and help.

Her major problem was fundraising, my area of strength. She was never being able to raise enough money to keep things ticking over and with the relentless introduction of needy donkeys on a weekly basis, things were getting fraught and desperate (I knew the feeling).

How could she set about getting better at raising funds? More importantly, could I advise her on how to do it? I was quick to explain that my case was different, as I worked with a circle of actors and actresses, performers who gave me an insight into their vulnerabilities and equally important, jobs. The generosity among busy, talented artists was sublime but for an outsider, there were the agents and managers to deal with, people who were employed for the sole purpose of dealing with the many requests asked of their clients and it was very rare for anyone from outside to get past them.

I warmed to Judy, as we talked. The Flicka Foundation was a very effective, attractive charity which was involved in some wonderful work with both rescuing horses and donkeys. It was in a lovely spot overlooking the sea and Falmouth harbour. I spent a day at Flicka but it was enough time for me to register what was going on and to understand the fundamental problems they faced. For example, there were not enough things to attract the public, of most importance, no brown signs, to let everyone know where they actually were. However, I could see immediately that they had a lot of donkeys and not an awful lot of room. As Judy explained, the council and relevant dignitaries had not rushed to their aid or their quest to enlarge and expand the project.

Arriving home, I couldn't get out of my mind that there was an association here that we might be able to combine the two. We could achieve this by closing down my sanctuary, moving all my donkeys down to Cornwall, let Flicka take over the strain and the work, leaving me to fundraise and make that side work as a success for them, alleviating their concerns for the future which was so evidently hanging over their heads, like a noose.

After a year of trials and tribulations, I made the change. We sold the farm and I made numerous journeys in a lorry to Cornwall, making sure they got every fence post, all the railings, saddles, bridles, tearoom chairs, and tables, everything that we had accumulated over twenty-nine years. At the end of those journeys, it was time to get the donkeys down which was done successfully, in four large horse boxes.

The donkeys immediately responded well to their new surroundings, making friends with the hundred or so donkeys that had been there for some time. Everything worked well. We were able to fight for and gain the farmhouse sale and give the proceeds to the foundation, so they had enough funds to take the extra animals that they had offered this wonderful home to. Also, the money took the financial pressure off them for a few years while everything sorted itself out.

Annie and I enjoyed our visits. As time went by, the donkeys recognised us a little less which we felt sad about but totally understood. We were always sad when Judy had to inform us that one of our beloved animals had passed away. We grieved for not being able to be there for our very special friends to pacify them and spend the last hours in their company. To be totally honest, we missed them terribly and the way of life we shared together. They were true and humble friends, incomparable to anything else.

We then set about starting our new life. Over the years since the new arrangement was set up, my talks have become established and although I focus on my stage and television career, I always finish with stories about the donkeys. The money we make goes, in part, to Flicka and we have achieved our goal on that score. Also, the audience around the country seem to be receptive to my dual career, they often find the donkeys more important than the artistic side which is gratifying in so many ways. I am able to enforce the truth about the cruelty still placed on these lovely animals and the situations they get into which is, in most part, not discussed or broached.

At the time of writing, the Flicka Foundation is going strong in Penryn, with more rescues. More grounds have been bought, two more big barns have been built and we have now constructed an animal hospital which is so vital to organisations like this, so all is well.

Hold no grudges

My final words must focus back onto the donkeys themselves and one in particular, Baz. He was the first donkey we ever rescued, the cornerstone of the whole empire he surveyed. He was the king of the herd, disciplining donkeys on the correct way to behave; teaching the foals how to grow up in a sizeable family; making sure the children with special needs got the attention they deserved; showing all around that to be allowed to lead a proper and contented life pays well for everyone.

Health-wise, he suffered from the lack of teeth. Just one in the front section was left but he still had his four back teeth. So, his friends pulled the grass up for him and left it lying around for him to gather, as pulling was now out of the question. He was still a good weight. The only regret our equine dentist had in life, was that he could not find a way of fixing Baz up with a pair of dentures!

Baz had been able to teach the donkeys that to hold a grudge wasn't the right way forward. No matter what had been done to them or what they had been put through, to remain dignified at all times was the answer and this he had portrayed to them all, by the way in which he had led his life, an example to make them think and reflect on.

Baz stepped in on fights on many occasions. He defended foals from over exuberant male donkeys trying to teach them a lesson. So many times, he also welcomed in sick donkeys and befriended them until they felt settled in the sanctuary.

Over his twenty-five years at the sanctuary, Baz had many admirers and solid relationships both with children and adults. He valued the attention and care those have shown him. He realised only too well that being our first donkey, he remained our pride and joy. He never ever let us down on any count whatsoever. We loved him very much as did so many others.

Baz had been sponsored by both Everton and Manchester United Football Clubs, although we tried not to let on to either, just in case of conflict or we lost their attentions! He was sponsored by Manchester Airport, Stepping Hill Hospital staff, 173 special needs schools, 43 adult learning centres, Sheffield Stroke Unit, 23 Women's Institutes, 12 Inner Wheel Clubs, 2 Golf Clubs, the Rotary Clubs and his pride and joy, the Variety Club of Great Britain, from whom he received our Variety Club bus. He was honoured by the island of Cyprus, the Liverpool Playhouse and so it went on. He was an extraordinary animal with extraordinary credentials.

It's the love Baz shared with everyone which was so inspiring. He just wanted to give. When Baz finally left it was difficult to imagine how life would carry on at the sanctuary, not just for the loss but the donkeys themselves, the children, the scene he had set, the standard he had maintained.

It was desperately sad when he left us but as with all the other donkeys that are no longer around, Baz will be remembered, always and remembered with much love.

Mary Berryman's
The Flicka Foundation
Horse & Donkey Sanctuary
Registered Charity No. 1153858

John and Annie Stirling support the Flicka Foundation,
a charity which has always ensured animals in their care,
and children in their need, are looked after with affection
for the rest of their lives.

We were so lucky to have found them when we did,
and we are so grateful that they took in all our donkeys
to give them such a lovely home and expert care.

Please support them if you can.

John and Annie Stirling

Flicka Foundation · Penty Noweth Farm · Trenoweth Lane
Mabe Burnhouse · Penryn · TR10 9JB
Tel: 01326 373601

Registered Charity No. 1153858

To Donate, please visit:
www.flickafoundation.org.uk/donate.html